MYANMAR
ARCHITECTURE
CITIES OF GOLD

Editor: Benny Chung

Designer: Jailani Basari

Production Coordinator: Nor Sidah Haron

Published by Times Editions – Marshall Cavendish

An imprint of Marshall Cavendish International (Asia) Private Limited

A member of Times Publishing Limited

Times Centre, 1 New Industrial Road, Singapore 536196

Tel: (65) 6213 9300   Fax: (65) 6285 4871

E-mail: te@sg.marshallcavendish.com

Online Bookstore: www.marshallcavendish.com/genref

Malaysian Office:

Marshall Cavendish (Malaysia) Sdn Bhd (3024-D)

(General & Reference Publishing)

(Formerly known as Federal Publications Sdn Bhd)

Times Subang

Lot 46, Persiaran Teknologi Subang

Subang Hi-Tech Industrial Park

Batu Tiga, 40000 Shah Alam

Selangor Darul Ehsan, Malaysia

Tel: (603) 5635 2191, 5628 6888   Fax: (603) 5635 2706

E-mail: cchong@my.marshallcavendish.com

National Library Board Singapore Cataloguing in Publication Data

Thanegi, Ma.

Myanmar Architecture : Cities of Gold – text by Ma Thanegi ; photographs by Barry Broman.

– Singapore : Times Editions-Marshall Cavendish, c2005.

p. cm.

Includes bibliographical references and index.

ISBN : 981-232-916-1

1. Architecture – Burma. 2. Vernacular architecture – Burma. 3. Historic buildings – Burma.

4. Burma – Civilization. I. Broman, Barry Michael, 1943- II. Title.

NA1512

720.9591 -- dc21   SLS2005015989

Printed in Singapore

MYANMAR
ARCHITECTURE
CITIES OF GOLD

Text by Ma Thanegi

Photographs by Barry Broman

Times Editions
Marshall Cavendish

For my late parents
U Tin Tut and Daw May Tin Tut,
with love. – Ma Thanegi

For Pappy. – Barry Broman

ACKNOWLEDGEMENTS

The author is greatly indebted to the untold number of Myanmar historians, writers and craftsmen who have contributed to Myanmar cultural history, for without their works she would have learnt little.

Her gratitude goes especially to Dr. Than Tun, Professor Emeritus for his engrossing books and articles; U Myo Myint Sein and team from the Rangoon Institute of Technology for their detailed research and drawings of traditional houses and old monasteries, and Tampawaddi U Win Maung and U Tin Win Myint of the Research Department, Ministry of Construction, for their findings on the *pyatthat* tiered roofs. Also, her heartfelt thanks to U Shwe Zan, patron of the Rakhine Thahaya Association, Yangôn, and U Tun Shwe Khaing, Rakhine scholar, for their in-depth studies of the pagodas of Mrauk Oo.

She is also grateful to all who helped with this project: U Ye Lin, for jump-starting it with copious notes, and architects Dr. Kyaw Lat and U Sun Oo, for their advice on many points.

Her special appreciation goes to U Sonny Nyein of Swiftwind Services, a friend, mentor and virtual database for all things Myanmar. She is as ever indebted to Clive Wing who many years ago taught her about the finer points of writing. To others too numerous to mention by name, go her grateful appreciation, always.

Any shortcomings are hers alone.

The photographer would like to mention a few of the people who have given so kindly of their time and cooperation. His special thanks to Major General Kyaw Win, U Ye Htoon, U Sein Myint, Daw Kyi Kyi Myint Toon, Patrick Robert and Claudia Saw Lwin, Marilyn Myers and U Soe Nyein.

INTRODUCTION

Hidden behind a socialist screen for nearly 30 years, Myanmar[1], known before 1989 as Burma, is the sleeping princess of Southeast Asia. The country is not without inner turmoil in her past, having had to endure 40 years of insurgency[2]. She has nonetheless escaped the bloody wars of the region, leaving her rich culture, steadfast traditions and hidden treasures, unseen by outsiders for many decades, intact.

Visitors began to return to Myanmar in the 1990s and, allowed access to regions once considered highly dangerous, they discovered ancient cultures still thriving in the country's vibrant music, delicate crafts and lively performing arts. Ruins of ancient cities, magnificent pagodas[3] and old-style teak mansions stand alongside beautiful colonial-era structures to form a tapestry of untold richness; a heritage preserved by strict isolation.

Myanmar has been so effectively hidden herself from the world that many are unaware of even her location. Approximately 261,228 square miles in size, the country lies between China and India, and shares her south-eastern border with Thailand. The western coastline faces the Bay of Bengal.

In upper Myanmar, the Chindwin River adds energy to the Ayeyarwady (Irrawaddy). The Ayeyarwady River itself runs like an artery through the centre of the country, passing through the mountainous regions of the north into the vast central plains, then onwards to a rich delta bordered by the Gulf of Mottama (Gulf of Martaban) and the Andaman Sea before finally spilling into the latter. While the Ayeyarwady is placid and has been used since ancient times for

irrigation and the transportation of goods and people, the Thanlwin (Salween) in the east is a wild, turbulent river. It is used for logging as its banks are lined with thick forests of teak.

Teak is not the sole natural resource of Myanmar. Some of the best rubies[4] in the world are produced in abundance from the mines of Mogok and the only imperial jade in the world comes from the Hpakant mines and a few other smaller mines in the Kachin State[5]. Sapphires of excellent quality and diamonds of a lesser grade are mined in the country as well. Gold dust and nuggets lie beneath the unpolluted waters of rivers and streams.

On this rich and fertile land live 135 national ethnicities. The majority is Bamar and the other main ethnic groups, each composed of various sub-ethnicities, are Shan, Chin, Kachin, Mon, Kayin, Rakhine and Kayah. Eighty-five per cent of the population is Buddhist and they live in harmony with the remaining 15 per cent[6]. Regardless of religious belief, the people are peaceful, content, friendly and hospitable.

For many years, it was believed that a group of people inhabiting what is now south-western China migrated eastwards into Myanmar around the fifth century B.C. However, recent palaeontological findings suggest that the Bamar ethnicity may be indigenous. Another possibility is that Tibeto-Burmese from south-eastern Tibet traversed the mountain ranges of what is now northern Myanmar to settle in the country.

Whatever their origin, archaeological evidence suggests that an early civilisation of people known as the Pyu had existed in Myanmar since the second century B.C. They founded the kingdoms of Halingyi, near present-day Shwebo; and Thayekhittaya (Sri Ksetra) and Beikthano, further south near Pyay (Prome). Another civilisation as ancient as the Pyu, if not more so, is the Rakhine. Also known as the Arakanese, they are a seafaring culture that has survived to this day. They live on a narrow strip of land on the western coast and their seaports were well known in the region. Their strong naval fleets once employed Portuguese mercenaries.

By the tenth century A.D., the Pyu kingdoms no longer existed and their people were assimilated into ethnic Bamar societies in 19 villages along the eastern banks of the Ayeyarwady. These villages later united to become the kingdom of Bagan (Pagan), seat of the first Burmese empire. The rise of Bagan also saw the rise of Theravada Buddhism, which remains the principal religion of the country.

After Bagan fell to the forces of Kublai Khan in the fourteenth century, a Shan-Bamar dynasty came to power and situated their capital at Inwa (Ava). Rising to power at about the same time was Bago (Pegu), a kingdom founded by the Mon in the thirteenth century, two centuries after the destruction of Thaton, capital of the Mon kingdom of Suvarnabhumi. These two kingdoms waged a war that lasted nearly

40 years. As both declined in power, exhausted by the futile battles that devastated their economies, the Bamar kingdom of Toungoo arose in the fifteenth century to conquer the Mon kingdom. Thus began the era of the second Burmese empire, founded by such great military kings as Tabinshwehti and Bayinnaung.

By the early eighteenth century, the British and the French had set up dockyards in a seaport in the Mon kingdom of Dagon, a place that was to become the modern capital of Myanmar, Yangôn (Rangoon). It had begun as a small village, made famous by the great Shwedagon Pagoda that had existed there, legends say, since the Buddha's lifetime over 2,500 years ago. The founder of the third Burmese empire, King Alaungpaya had annexed the land from the Mon kingdom in 1755 and renamed the town Yangôn, or "End of Strife".

Tension with British settlers following a minor border dispute led to the outbreak of the First Anglo-Burmese War in 1824. At the end of the war two years later, Burma had lost Rakhine on the western coast and Taninthayi (Tenasserim) on the southern coast to the British.

The Second Anglo-Burmese War broke out in 1852. After the war, the British annexed all of lower Burma, including Yangôn. This period produced a rich diversity of architectural styles, an exotic fusion of east and west. Buildings that exhibit these styles still exist in many places,

In the nineteenth century, both the French and the British had set their eyes on the lucrative natural resources and trade routes of Burma, and their race for monopoly culminated in the Third Anglo-Burmese War of 1885. The last king of Burma, Thibaw was sent into exile after the British seized the whole country and declared it a province of India. It was only in 1948 that Burma finally regained her independence.

Pagodas, ruined temples and old monasteries remain as relics of Myanmar's past, their styles and histories reflecting the religious, social, political and economic environments of their time. Stories about how they came to be built are intertwined with the fascinating histories of their respective donors. Buildings in Myanmar can thus be classified according to four categories:

a) Ancient structures from the Pyu, Rakhine and Bagan civilisations
b) Traditional buildings from the time of the Burmese kings
c) Vernacular architecture for religious and secular buildings
d) Colonial architecture with British influences

Now, as Myanmar discards her cloak of mystery and steps into a fast-paced, modern world, it is time to take pleasure in her ancient cities of gold, elegant traditional architecture, and grand old buildings

ANCIENT CIVILISATIONS

Thayekhittaya:
Lost City of the Pyu Kingdom

A few ruined temples that date back to around the second century stand near the town of Pyay (Prome) and on another site 80 miles away. They were built by the Pyu kingdoms of Thayekhittaya (Sri Ksetra) and Beikthano. Both kingdoms had flourished in the second century B.C., reaching the height of their glory between the fourth and the ninth centuries. Thayekhittaya conquered Beikthano and was itself probably destroyed in A.D. 832 by invaders from Nanchao, now Yunnan province in China, as noted by the ninth-century Chinese scholar Fan Cha'o in his text, *Manshu*.

Within a few decades, the gentle Pyu had vanished. A pious people, they left monuments to their faith in temples that today stand in empty fields. The delicate and intricate workmanship of their crafts serve as testaments to their creativity and highly cultured nature. Charmingly diplomatic, they left evidence of their culture in relics such as finely-wrought jewellery and the records of the Chinese, with whom they had often exchanged cultural missions.

Fan Cha'o wrote that before Thayekhittaya was plundered it had been encircled by a wall covered in glazed green tiles. The city had hundreds of monasteries for Buddhist monks "with courts and rooms all decked out with gold and silver, coated with cinnabar and bright colours,

smeared with kino and covered with embroidered rugs". The people were "... peaceful, courteous and charming. There is a great white image a hundred feet in height that they worship. Both boys and girls reaching age seven shave their head and become novices at monasteries and nunneries. On reaching 20, those who do not wish to enter the Order can return to secular life. Gold and silver are used as money, the shape of which is crescent-like. They have a variety of musical instruments including the phoenix-headed harp with 14 strings, the crocodile-headed zither with nine strings, the dragon-headed lute with three running pegs and frets, and many kinds of drums. Both men and women wear silk-like fine cotton, for they would not wear silk as it involved the taking of life".

According to *pa-sat yarza win*, or "verbal history", Thayekhittaya, located near Pyay, had once been ruled by King Duttabaung and Beikthano, about 80 miles further north, by the beautiful Princess Pantra. Myths tell of the vengeance of Pantra against King Duttabaung who had captured the princess and made her his queen. King Duttabaung had loved her deeply, it is said, but she felt only bitter hatred for the one who had conquered her. Through witchery, she took away the glory of the king, which was centred in his third eye, and his kingdom fell into decline. Both monarchs were descended from the dynasty that ruled the lost city of Tagaung, which lay further north. Tales of their ancestry are filled with characters such as a powerful magical serpent and his lover the queen, a simple cowherd who became king, his twin sons blinded from birth, a beautiful ogress who restored their sight and a fairy girl born of a deer. With such magical ancestry, it seems natural that the Pyu should have been people of great talent and skill.

Pyu artefacts found at the sites of the old cities include 20 sheets of gold inscribed with Buddhist texts; Buddha images and statuettes of musicians and dancers in cast metal; gold animal figurines; burial urns of clay and beads of gold, amber and agate, some in the form of animals such as elephants. There was also fine repoussé silver work and gold jewellery of such intricate and delicate detail that they would shame modern craftsmen with their state-of-the-art tools. Additionally, there were milky agates the size of peas, probably used as seals, with minute but detailed animal figures and letters cut into them. A bead

six inches long had a bore along its length so narrow that it could take only the finest of silk threads.

The few buildings left are all religious in nature as secular buildings and even palaces were presumably constructed of wood, a style that was to remain in succeeding centuries. The pieces of bricks found scattered around Thayekhittaya have ridges, formed by pressing fingers in the still-wet clay, and, more rarely, details of figures and etchings of numbers and letters.

Phaya Gyi Pagoda, with a conical shape that would eventually evolve into the standard pagoda stupa[7] of today, is a structure topped with a gold-plated filigree *hti*, or "umbrella", an inverted cone with a bejewelled banner at its apex[8]. Bawbawgyi Pagoda is a 153-foot-high cylindrical stupa crowned by a small dome. Its hollow interior rises to about two-thirds its height and has an opening at the base.

The stupas of this period are basically Indian in form, with the sides rising in a straight line. A typical Burmese design, based on the shape of a bell with the bottom edge flaring slightly upwards, would emerge by the eleventh century.

Two pagodas of the temple type, in the form of cave structures known as *gu*[9], are the Bebe and the Lemyethna[10] temples. The Bebe is a square building surmounted by a rounded dome with a porch that opens towards the east. It features voussoir brickwork and radiating arches, precursors to the architecture of eleventh-century Bagan temples. The same workmanship can be seen in Lemyethna Temple.

Little is known about the passing of the Pyu kingdoms. Whatever may have happened, few of its people survived. However, traces of the Pyu do remain; their language in a few inscriptions, their culture in delicate crafts, their faith in their temples and their lives in legends[11].

Pages 14–15: *Ruined Pyu structures such as this dot the landscape near Prome.*

Left: *Bawbawgyi Pagoda, like Phaya Gyi Pagoda, lies outside the city walls of Thayekhittaya, being south of the city itself.*

Right: *Phaya Gyi Pagoda, located northwest of the city walls of the ancient Pyu city of Thayekhittaya.*

Mrauk U:
Golden Capital of the Western Coast

Greek geographer Ptolemy's second-century records of the sea routes between China and east Asia mention a country called "Argyre", later identified by scholars as Arakan, the Rakhine State. The fifteenth-century Venitian merchant Niccolò de' Conti wrote the name as "Rachani", while mid-sixteenth-century Turkish geographer Sidi Ali Chelebi used the name "Rakanj". The term "Aracan" was first used by Barbosa in 1516 in *The Book of Duarte Barbosa*. Michael Symes, the first British emissary to the Burmese kingdom, wrote about visiting the western coastal country of the "Yee-Kein". It was a rich kingdom, being one of the most important ports in the region. Historical accounts also mention the existence of silver mines in the country.

The Rakhine civilisation was contemporary with the rise of the Pyu kingdoms but long mountain ranges effectively formed a barrier between the two. Little is known or recorded about their interchange. Both used silver coinage, a monetary system that fell into disuse in central Myanmar from the end of Pyu rule until the eighteenth century when it was reintroduced by King Bodawpaya.

The last of the great cities of Rakhine, Mrauk U was founded in the year 1430 after several others had been abandoned in turn. Astrology plays a part almost equal to politics in Myanmar history and cities were often relocated merely to avert unhappy fates foretold in the calculations of men learned in the art of prophecy.

The prosperous city enjoyed trade with kingdoms of the Middle East as well as the Far East and became an important port of call. Wouter Schouten, a Dutchman who saw the port in the seventeenth century remarked that it was the richest in Asia, comparable to ports such as Amsterdam and London. Persian and Arabic inscriptions found on stone surfaces provide evidence of its far-reaching trade ties.

The rulers of Mrauk U had strong naval fleets that counted the service of hundreds of Portuguese mercenaries. By a strange twist of fate and politics, a number of samurai fleeing imperial wrath in Japan

Right: *Dukkhan Thein Pagoda, located in Mrauk U, is a massive stone and mortar building.*

in 1623 arrived in Mrauk U and were recruited to serve as the Rakhine king's personal bodyguards.

Since the early sixteenth century, frequent wars had broken out between the Rakhine and the Burmese of upper Myanmar, as well as the Mon who inhabited the delta. The Rakhine conquered the Mon kingdom in 1599 and carried off, among other treasures, the Khmer statues that the Mon had looted from Siam, which Siamese armies had earlier taken from the Khmer kingdom of Angkor. In 1785, the statues were again seized as war booty from Mrauk U by a Crown Prince from the Kingdom of Inwa in upper Myanmar. Also taken was the most-prized possession of the Rakhine, the 12-foot-7-inch-high bronze Mahamuni Image of the Buddha said to have been blessed by the Buddha himself.

The image was enshrined in Mandalay and devotees have since applied so much gold leaf to it that the statue has lost all proportion in its torso and limbs. The Khmer statues are also kept in Mandalay on the platform of the Mahamuni Pagoda. Until the 1960s when a pavilion was erected for them, the Khmer statues had been standing in open air and fettered with iron chains: people say they kept trying to escape. Most of the pilgrims who visited the pagoda believed the statues, not knowing their actual home was in another country, wanted to return to Mrauk U. The statues, including one of a three-headed elephant, are not there just for show; pilgrims rub parts of their bodies to heal ills in their own. The statues' bronze heads, chests, abdomens and knees shine with daily rubbings as they have reputedly been curing the population for centuries.

Father Sebastien Manrique, a Portuguese missionary of the Augustinian Order who arrived in Rakhine in the mid seventeenth century recorded in his *Travels* what he saw one January morning in 1635: "... the sun rose... bringing to life the gilded roofs which flashed as if they were made of gold... the Hall of Audience, which was carved with much fancy, was supported by a forest of gilt and red lacquer pillars". This was Mrauk U.

Right: *The resplendent Mahamuni Pagoda in Mandalay houses the famed Mahumani Buddha and bronze Khmer statues pictured in the following pages.*

Manrique described in detail the architecture and interior of the Royal Palace, that it had "massive wooden columns of such extraordinary length and straightness that one wonders there are trees so tall and straight... the inside columns are entirely gilt... these places also contain rooms made of fragrant wood such as white and red sandalwood. In those apartments the sense of smell has its special delight... there is a hall gilt from top to bottom which they call the Golden House because it has a vine of pure gold which occupies the whole roof of the hall, with a hundred odd *combalengas*[12] of the same pure gold... in breadth and shaped like big pumpkins... each one of them weighs ten *viss*[13] or 40 pounds Spanish".

He also noted that the residences of princes and lords had "rooms made of wood with different sculptures and mouldings of woodwork being gilt and painted in various colours". The houses of common people meanwhile were built of "fine variegated mats, very neat and beautiful things... without any kind of nailing... using ligaments of reeds". Manrique also mentioned the "*basars*[14] where all sorts of commodities were sold". The perfumed pavilions, gilded roofs and scarlet pillars Manrique described have all since disappeared. The only record that remains of the people who once lived in Mrauk U is the figures etched in relief on temple walls.

Religious architecture in Mrauk U is distinctive, as the buildings seem to have been constructed for defence as well. Some historians believe that in addition to being places of worship, they may have also served as lookout posts. Certainly, Mrauk U was a well-fortified city. Maurice Collis[15] visited the ruins in 1924 and saw "a meander of lakes and moats, which wound in and out, sometimes one behind the other, with blind alleys, false entrances backed with high stone battlements, and escarpments formed out of existing ridges... also, three huge reservoirs... which could be opened to flood the lower town".

The images in Mrauk U too have a distinctly different style. The torsos are of massive build, the jaws square and the features almost voluptuous, unlike Burmese or Shan images, which are slender and graceful and have delicate features. Some stucco and stone decorative motifs have arabesque influences that make them look vastly different from the floral **Kanote** designs of the Burmese or Shan. Although similarities to Burmese designs may be observed in the motifs on

Left: *The disproportionate image of the Mahamuni Buddha.*

Opposite and below: *The famous bronze Khmer statues at Mahamuni Pagoda. For hundreds of years, people have rubbed various parts of the statues to cure their ailments.*

arches that serve as the foundations for tiered roofs or as the tops for doorways, typical Rakhine styles are also incorporated. This is evident in the stone façades of the Laung Ban Pyauk Pagoda and the Kado Thein[16], the latter of which lies in Launggret, an older capital some miles away from Mrauk U. Through this fusion of creative styles, Rakhine architects created a harmonious union of grace and strength.

A structure representative of the hundreds of temples in the Rakhine State is the Shitthaung Pagoda, "The Eighty-thousand", in Mrauk U built by King Minbargyi (r. 1531–1553) in 1535. Also called Minbin, the king was the most powerful ruler of his dynastic line. Because he built the pagoda after successfully repelling an attack by the Portuguese, it was also known as Yan Aung Zeya, "The Pagoda of Victory". "The Eighty-thousand" actually refers to the number of gold images he had enshrined in the treasure chamber beneath the foundations of the temple.

Built entirely of sandstone without any cement, this cave temple measures 160 feet long, 124 feet wide and 86 feet high. It is surmounted by a stupa, with 26 smaller stupas around it. Walls nine feet thick and 12 feet high line the upper platform on the west and south. Along the northern and southern walls is a line of brick stupas, the gaps between them bridged by stone slabs covered with relief figures on both sides. They include the head of a bull projecting out of the stone slab, celestial beings, a cobra with hood spread and a lotus blossom in its fangs, an ogre and other mythical creatures such as the *By'lar,* a creature combining the parts of nine different animals[17] which is native to the Rakhine State and not found in other parts of Myanmar.

The inner walls of the temple consist of more than a thousand stone slabs carved with six tiers of figures in bas-relief. The upper tiers show scenes from the *Jataka* tales[18] and images of the Buddha-to-be in his earlier incarnations as birds and animals. Figures of the donor, King Minbargyi, and his queens as well as celestial beings and ogres appear in their own tiers. The sarongs worn by the ladies feature many designs, including the typical Burmese wavy-line *Acheik* pattern.

The images standing in the corners have more than two arms, revealing a Hindu influence. The lowest tier shows the sports, dances and gymnastics of the country, including the military training of men and war elephants. Some scenes show men practising martial arts using swords, lances and staves. One section shows the sport of *kyin* wrestling, which is still practised by Rakhine men. In the last passage

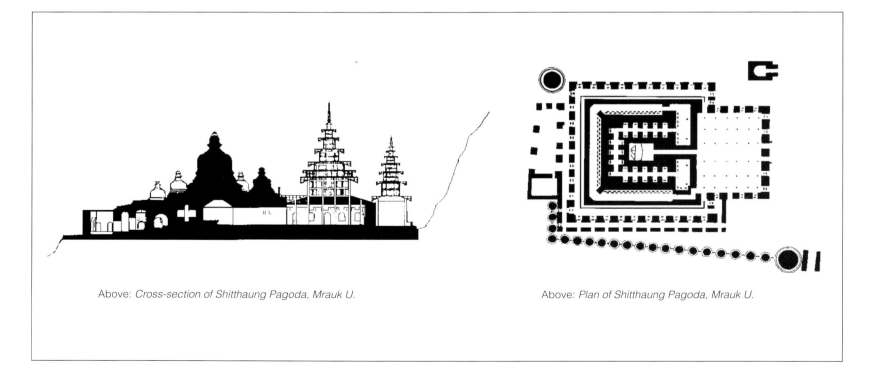

Above: *Cross-section of Shitthaung Pagoda, Mrauk U.*

Above: *Plan of Shitthaung Pagoda, Mrauk U.*

is the footprint of the Buddha in a rarely seen style; the sole is plain, without any of the 108 markings.

When King Minbargyi's son, King Digra, ascended the throne, court astrologers told him that he had only six months to live; if he wanted to prolong his life, he would have to build a pagoda with the noble number of nine. Thus it came to be that in 1553, Digra, also called Min Theikkha, built the Koethaung Pagoda, "The Ninety-thousand". It is the biggest pagoda in Mrauk U, measuring 230 feet by 250 feet. People to this day believe that Digra was trying to surpass his father, the man who built "The Eighty-thousand".

Digra was assassinated before the pagoda was finished, although he lived for three years more instead of the prophesied six months. No one bothered to finish building the pagoda and when it was finally excavated in the 1980s, roof tiles were found stacked in a neat pile still awaiting installation by long-dead workmen.

The Dukkhan Thein, built by King Minphalaung (r. 1571–c. 1593), is also a massive building of stone and mortar. It measures 190 feet from north to south and 200 feet from east to west. A gloomy, spiralling inner passage running across two tiers leads to an inner chamber. One hundred and forty-six niches are set along the length of this passage, each containing the stone image of a seated Buddha. Along the vaulted passages, there are carved figures. These include 64 ladies, each of whom sports a different hairstyle, preserving for the study of present-day scholars a record of fashion in the Rakhine Kingdom during the sixteenth century.

The Andaw[19] Thein is the temple housing the Buddha tooth relic. It is an octagonal structure. Set on a high platform is the main stupa, which is surrounded by eight smaller ones. The temple is about 40 feet high and has a roof ten feet thick. The whole structure is again surrounded by smaller pagodas. It was built in 1521 by King Min Hla Raza and the original pagoda was encased when it was rebuilt in 1596 by King Min Raza Gree.

A rectangular prayer hall leads to the main chamber, which is octagonal. There are two inner corridors in the chamber with 142 images set in niches along the walls of the outer corridor. The central pillar is octagonal. Each side holds a Buddha image in a domed niche. The images show the Buddha's robe tied at the chest. The Buddhist

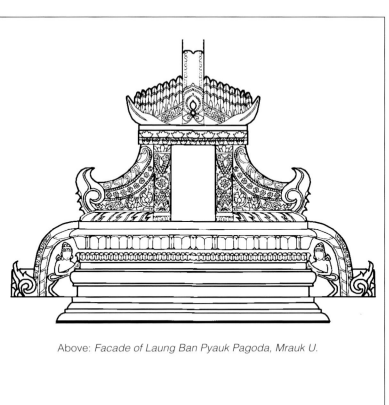

Above: *Facade of Laung Ban Pyauk Pagoda, Mrauk U.*

Above: *Facade of Kado Thein, Launggret.*

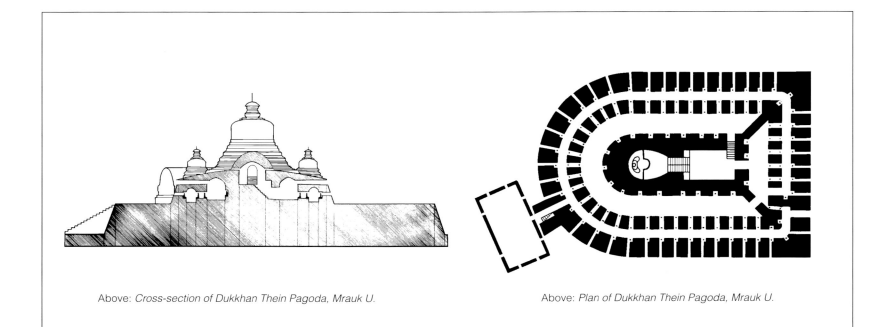

Above: *Cross-section of Dukkhan Thein Pagoda, Mrauk U.*

Above: *Plan of Dukkhan Thein Pagoda, Mrauk U.*

Above: *Facade of the Andaw Thein in Mrauk U showing Hindu deities at the base of its columns.*

belief is that the robes were tied such to keep them in place when Buddha and his attendant monks travelled through the air. Figures of a minister holding an umbrella, a *Kinnara* birdman, a king and Ganesh, the Hindu elephant-headed God, stand at each corner of the central pillar, between the images of the Buddha.

The façade of Andaw Thein also shows Hindu deities in postures of support to Buddha. In Myanmar, as in many other parts of Asia, deities of other religions are neither scorned nor ignored but often assimilated to form an all-embracing pantheon symbolising peace and harmony within different beliefs.

The Rakhine are traditionally skilled in the casting of bronze images. Many are depicted wearing crowns[20] and royal raiment and are known as *Maha Kyain,* or "Royal Oath", images. Each time a new king ascended the throne, an image depicting him in his coronation regalia would be made. It was a crucial part of the coronation for the king to swear to uphold his ten kingly duties[21] while holding the image on his head. Such images would later be enshrined at a pagoda where people involved in disputes gathered to swear their oaths.

By the eighteenth century, the kingdom of Rakhine had fallen to the Burmese king; and when the Burmese in turn lost to the British in the First Anglo-Burmese War of 1824, Rakhine was ceded to the British Crown. The British moved the capital that once covered an area of 25 square miles to a tiny fishing village 45 miles away called Sittway[22], "Where War Was Seen".

Left: *The gilded image of a* nat *rests at the bottom of a stupa in Mrauk U.*

Bottom: *This statue of an ogre with a fearsome visage stands guard at a temple in Sittway.*

Bagan:
Kingdom of Four Thousand Temples

The ruined temples, pagodas and monasteries of Bagan[23], a kingdom that flourished between the tenth and fourteenth centuries, stand on the wide, flat plains of central Myanmar. Although contemporary Mon records described the place as a "parched" region, it was a land of greatness and wealth, being the capital of the first Burmese empire. At present, only a few villages remain as keepers of that heritage, guarded by images of brother and sister nat[24] set in two alcoves on either side of the Tharapa Gate.

The male nat is Min Mahagiri, or "Lord of the Mountain". He had in life been a blacksmith of great strength and was burned to death by a king. His sister had earlier been made a queen, the easier to trap him when he visited her. As he burned, she too jumped into the fire. They became nat and were worshipped as guardians of homes and the city. Villagers still offer fresh flowers at their shrines even though the city they once protected has long since disappeared.

More than a thousand years ago, Bagan would have bustled with people at work and play, colourful royal processions and pompous nobles in parade. The air would have been joyful with the tinkling of bells attached to the harnesses of horses and cattle as well as the creaking of wheels. According to folklore, a code in the rhyme "Sweet sounds are heard, from wheels of carts,"[25] reveals that there were once 4,446 temples in Bagan. The number is probably accurate as today, ten centuries later, 2,230 remain[26], scattered on 16 square miles of parched, hot and dry plains. It is the dry earth that contributes to the strong sweetness of the sap of the toddy palm[27], which remains a foundation of Bagan economy to this day. The Bagan Kingdom encompassed paddy fields to the north, made fertile with canals, dams and man-made lakes. The kings of Bagan made sure that enough rice was grown for the people of their parched land.

Left: *One of the reputed four thousand temples in Bagan.*

The Bagan era saw the establishment of Buddhism across the whole country, the refining of the Burmese language and the creation of arts and crafts still practised today. It was a Golden Age, but the golden palaces, like the huts of the poor, have since disappeared. Only temples of brick and stone remain. Most of the bigger temples have been maintained through the ages with funding from donations made by the masses or the patronage of reigning monarchs. Although Bagan as a city is no more, these monuments have served as living sites of worship for centuries.

According to local chronicles, these temples dedicated to the establishment of the peaceful philosophy of Theravada Buddhism owe their beginnings to violence and destruction. The 42nd king of the Bagan dynasty, Anawrahta (r. 1044–1077), also known as Aniruddha, carried the country to greatness through military might and religious fervour.

It is said that during his rule, King Anawrahta had grown uneasy with the growing power of an animistic sect led by Ari priests and their practices, which were driven by superstition and fear. Although the people had been both Theravada and Mahayana Buddhist[28] devotees since centuries past, the Ari priests were gaining too many converts among the lower classes and their practices getting too unsavoury. The king wanted to establish the True Word at all levels of society. When a monk named Shin Arahan from the southern Mon country of Suvarnabhumi came to Bagan, King Anawrahta heard of the complete texts of Theravada Buddhism in the hands of the Mon king, Manuha. King Anawrahta was determined to get copies and urgently dispatched ambassadors to Suvarnabhumi.

Suvarnabhumi, the Golden Land of the Mon, had its capital at Thaton, situated a few miles inland from the seaport of Martaban. Martaban later became one of the capitals of the Mon kingdom but, even as a mere port, it was always an important trade centre for coastal kingdoms stretching from the Middle East to the Far East. The port city traded in oils, spices and the popular Martaban jars, bulbous glaze-ware with tapering bases made by Mon potteries.

Right: *A devotee makes offerings to a* nat
at the Shwezigon Pagoda, Bagan.

King Manuha, being the ruler of such a cultured land, considered the people of Bagan to be mere barbarians. With contempt, he refused to hand over the texts. King Anawrahta then invaded the Mon, conquered Thaton and carried off the king and the royal family as prisoners. He also took the complete set of Buddhist texts as well as thousands of artisans and craftsmen.

King Manuha, who was said to have been brought to Bagan in shackles of gold, was allowed to sell his ruby ring to a rich farmer for six cartloads of silver. He used the funds to build a temple, with a prayer that in future incarnations, he would never again live as another man's prisoner. The temple, named after him, houses four immense Buddha statues, three in the sitting posture and one reclining, in spaces so restrictively narrow that worshippers might feel the depths of King Manuha's despair. Thousands of temples stand on the vast plains of Bagan, but certainly none have this ambience of sorrow.

Below: Manuha Pagoda in Bagan, built by a Mon king of the same name who had been imprisoned after the founder of the first Myanmar empire, Anawrahta, invaded his kingdom.

Opposite: Various statues of the Buddha in Bagan. The reclining statue of the Buddha on the bottom left is one of four at Manuha Pagoda. Note the low ceilings that contribute toward the cramped atmosphere.

It was during King Anawrahta's reign that construction on the temples of Bagan began, but in Thaton and elsewhere in Mon, no such buildings stand. The architects of the temples seem to have been native sons of Bagan, although there are designs and paintings with Indian or Mon influences. Some scholars question the whole story, as there are no contemporary records[29].

As Buddhism grew more established, the building of monuments dedicated to this religion also began. King Anawrahta fashioned votive tablets with his own hands[30], incised with two lines of prayer proclaiming that, desiring to be free of *samsara*[31], the Great King Aniruddha himself made the image of the Lord. His votive tablets had been found at sites from Katha in the north down to Twante of the delta, near present-day Yangôn. His passing at the age of 75 was mysterious; it was said that he was out riding alone when he was gored to death by a spirit disguised as a buffalo and that his body was taken away by celestials.

The earliest temples of Bagan were evidently styled after the Bebe and Lemyethna temples of Thayekhittaya. They have a basic square shape with the Buddha image set against the far wall opposite the main entrance. The interior darkness is relieved only by a few perforated windows. It is believed that such temples were meant for meditation instead of worship. The art of using voussoired bricks to make vaulting and radiating arches was perfected at the temples of Bagan.

Opposite: *Dozens of temples dot the plains of Bagan.*

Left: *Detail of a building in Bagan showing intricate stuccowork.*

A later period of temple architecture incorporates what is known as Old Mon style, mainly because inscriptions at the temples built in this style were found to be in the Mon language despite the fact that Burmese writing also existed at the time. Temples in the Old Mon style generally have one main hall leading to an inner chamber with a square central shrine. A corridor runs around the core and images appear on each of its four sides. A few perforated brick windows with lattices of stone or terracotta let in faint gleams of light, the better to preserve the colours of the murals and to invoke a sense of awe and piety in worshippers. Staircases leading to the upper levels would be hidden in the thick walls.

Entrances to the temple are usually set in the three outer walls of the front hall but in smaller temples, only one front entrance would be built. The interior would still remain dark, with the corridor lit by perforated windows, to give the worshipper a sense of detachment from the outside world. Usually, the core would contain a relic chamber, where relics of the Buddha, jewels, images and other donated articles would presumably have been placed before it was sealed. The huge Buddha images enshrined inside the temples were usually built out of bricks or mortar, as marble is not found in the region. The use of these materials allowed for more treasures to be enshrined in the head, upper arms and the abdomen[32].

Examples of these early temples, in which the use of decorative motifs may differ, include the Myinkaba Gubyaukgyi with it exquisite murals, the Wetkyi-in Gubyaukgyi, the Apeyadana Temple, the Pahtothamya Temple and the Nagayon, "Embraced by the Dragon". The last of these, the Nagayon, has a huge image of the Buddha sheltered by the hood of a *naga*, or dragon. The image symbolises the time that the Buddha, having just attained enlightenment, sat by Muncalinda Lake to meditate. During a storm, the *naga*, which lived in the lake, rose out of the waters to wrap its coils around the Buddha and flare its hood over his head in protection. This scene, often used for Buddha images, sometimes gives visitors the false impression that the images are symbols of snake worship.

The exterior walls of these temples are decorated with detailed stuccos of scrolls, friezes and carvings of stylised flora, called *Kanote* flowers, interspersed with mythical creatures. An ogre, depicted with hands clutching at falling strands of flowers or beads spilling out of either side of its mouth, is a popular motif and is called *Belu Pan Hswai* or "Ogre Clutching Flowers". Other motifs are *Kinnara* bird-people bearing lotuses, lions with flame-like manes and snake dragons with hoods flared and fangs bared. Information about the constituents for the mortar used to create these decorative motifs has been handed down through the generations in a verse[33].

Many temples have murals painted on ceilings and walls. These mostly feature scenes from the *Jataka* or the Buddha's life story. Scenes of secular life are rarely depicted in the earlier paintings. Most of them have Indian influences in the face or form, and some feature Hindu deities, the result of the commercial and social intercourse that existed between the two countries at that time and the accommodating attitude the people had toward the co-existence of different religions. Some temples, such as the Apeyadana built by King Kyansittha's queen, have wall paintings incorporating Mahayana Buddhist figures of Avalokiteasvara, a *Bodhisattva* or Future Buddha. Paintings in the Paya Thonzu and Nandamanya temples also featured deities belonging to Tantric, or mystical, Mahayana Buddhism.

A later style of architecture categorised as the Late Mon emerged in the early part of the twelfth century[34]. An example is the beautiful Ananda Temple built in 1105 by King Kyansittha (r. 1084–c. 1112), the first elected king in Myanmar history.

The Ananda has three levels of sloping roofs followed by three receding terraces. It is crowned by a grooved, curvilinear tower. A small stupa crowned with a *hti* surmounts the tower. The arch-pediments protrude slightly from the vestibules with stuccos of flame-like motifs soaring from the top. Four panels on each side of the tower each contain a vertical row of five niches with seated images of the Buddha.

A unique aspect of the Ananda is its use of stone and brick, the latter made of baked clay and paddy husks, in alternating segments to reinforce the strength of its archways, the earliest example of this use.

The floor plan is a perfect Greek cross with the centre dominated by a square main shrine. An inner and outer corridor run along the perimeter of the shrine. These two dark corridors are lined with 1,447 glazed terracotta plaques depicting the *Jataka* stories and the armies of Maya the Evil One. The story of Gautama Buddha's life, from his birth to his death, is set in 142 stone slabs in detailed relief. Lines of Mon script on each tablet explain each scene.

The four arms of the cross form long corridors that lead towards the 31-foot-5-inch-high gilded standing images. The images, each made of different materials, are enshrined in the arched alcoves on each side of the central pillar in the standard cardinal points. They represent the four Buddhas who have already graced the world: Kakusanda in the north, Konagamana in the east, Kassapa in the south, and Gautama, the last, in the west.

Originally, the northern image was of champac wood, the eastern of teak, the southern of pine and the western of a combination of five metals, also known as *pyinsa law*, that included silver and gold. Only the northern and southern images are original as the western image was melted down for the gold by desecraters at an unknown period and replaced in the late nineteenth century by a merchant from Bagan. Its pedestal is the original, cast from five metals. The eastern image burnt down accidentally and was replaced in the nineteenth century by the governor of Bagan, an official of the royal court of Mandalay.

Small images of Shin Arahan and King Kyansittha are shown in postures of obeisance at the foot of the last Buddha, Gautama, in the western shrine. The images of the monk and the king are made of gilded lacquer, proof that the famous craft of Bagan had existed since King Kyansittha's time[35]. Corridors also run along the first storey. Strategically placed openings along these higher corridors let in shafts of light that beam down on the kindly faces of the Buddhas.

Opposite: *Detail of the flame-like arch-pediments over the entrances of Ananda Temple in Bagan.*

Below: *Ananda Temple, built by King Kyansittha in the early twelfth century.*

Right: *One of the images of the Buddha housed in Ananda Temple.*

Although no palaces remain, King Kyansittha did leave a stone inscription[36] in Mon describing the new one he constructed in 1101, 17 years into his reign. The work, which began on 4 November 1101 with a ceremonial cleansing of the site by Brahmin astrologers, was completed on 9 May 1102. The simple palace plan consisted of a large central hall with four smaller pavilions on each side, all five structures roofed with the *pyatthat*[37]. The carvings and decorations of the eaves, pillars, gates and doors were marvellous in detail and embellishment[38]. Elaborate rituals were performed to accompany each process in the construction of the palace, and exact and auspicious measurements had to be calculated for the cutting of timber.

The end of King Kyansittha's reign marked a vital point for historians. The king did not choose his son, Rajakumar, to succeed him. Rather, the crown was passed to Alaungsithu, who was his grandson and Rajakumar's nephew. Nevertheless, out of love and filial piety, Rajakumar built the Myinkaba Gubyaukgyi Temple and dedicated it to King Kyansittha, who succumbed to a fatal illness at the age of 72. He also erected a stone pillar[39] with the dedication to his father inscribed in four languages: Pyu, Pali, Mon and Burmese.

The pillar was a priceless legacy for scholars as it enabled them to decipher the Pyu stone inscriptions of Bagan and gain insight into the society which existed at that time. The inscriptions included records of court cases, writings commemorating the building of temples by donors, lists of items and slaves donated to pagodas; and lists of officials and scholars at court, some of whom were women. Village leaders were sometimes women, and queens and princesses held great power behind the scenes. The legends of great kings such as Anawrahta and Kyansittha spoke of romances with queens and princesses who were as beautiful as they were politically astute.

A later type of architecture, known as the Burmese style because it developed simultaneously with the Burmese language, incorporated open, arched doorways and windows that let in ample light and air. Some of these structures were double-storeyed. In these, the vaults were staggered so that there is a marked reduction in weight and amount of building materials used. Flat terraces replaced the sloping roof. Smaller bricks were used, the true voussoir arch was developed and stone began to be more commonly added to strengthen buildings. Examples of Burmese-style architecture include the Sulamani, Gawdawpalin and Htilominlo Temples.

A temple bridging the transition of the Mon to the Burmese style is the Thatbyinnyu or "Omniscience of the Buddha". The Ananda is often considered the most beautiful temple and the Dhammayangyi the most impressive but the Thatbyinnyu is surely the most splendid of all. It was the first, and the highest, of the double-storeyed temples to be built.

Thatbyinnyu Temple was the merit of King Kyansittha's grandson and successor, King Alaungsithu (r. 1113–1167). He was a greatly-loved king who supposedly travelled far and wide, apparently on a magic barge, and almost any old pagoda discovered in any imaginable part of the country is attributed to him.

Thatbyinnyu was completed around 1144, at the height of King Alaungsithu's reign. It rises to 201 feet with square flat terraces that narrow towards a curvilinear stupa topped by a tapering spire. The temple is two storeys high with two floors on each storey. The proportions of the two square forms set one on the other, with the corner cubicles capped by small stupas on the receding terraces, make this majestic structure seem as if it soars into the clouds.

The entrances to the temple have arch-pediments rising like tongues of flames. The main entrance faces east with wide steps leading towards a corridor running around the four sides of the central shrine. The wide central stairway on the eastern side leads to the upper storey where parallel corridors run around the central block. Two stairways lead to the terrace on top of the vestibule. A central stairway leads upwards to the second storey where the main image of the temple is enshrined in a vaulted chamber. Two narrow flights of stairs built in the thick walls also lead to this image. Large windows and doors graced with bold arch-pediments admit bright light and cool breezes.

An earlier temple, built by King Alaungsithu in 1131, the Shwegugyi was also a change from the darker temples of the Mon style. It is known as Nan Oo Paya or "The Temple at the Head of the Palace". Excavations indeed found the palace site next to this structure.

The Shwegugyi is much smaller than the Thatbyinnyu but has a delicate elegance of its own. It has windows and doors in the central hall and along the corridors so that the interior enjoys ample light and air. An inscription in Pali verse records King Alaungsithu's prayer that by this merit might he be reborn in the time of Meitara, the Buddha for whom the world waits, and that "informed by such a Teacher, I (would) also become a Buddha in the eyes of spirits and men...". It was in this temple that Alaungsithu, a well-loved king, was smothered to death at the age of 101 by his son Narathu.

Although the Burmese character of the pagoda plan was well established at the time, King Narathu (r. 1167–1170) reverted to the Late Mon style when he built the Dhammayangyi Temple. Despite their both being of the same style, the Dhammayangyi is so massive that it seems the opposite of the delicate Ananda.

Opposite: *Detail of a woodcarving at Sale Monastery, south of Bagan.*

Far left: *The impressive-looking Thatbyinnyu Temple, merit of King Alaungsithu.*

Left: *Close-up of an image of the Buddha at Thatbyinnyu Temple.*

During the construction of Dhammayangyi, King Narathu was murdered by assassins under the instruction of an Indian prince whose daughter he had killed. He went down in history as Kala-kya Min, "The King Felled by the Indians", and the temple was left incomplete.

The outer walls of Dhammayangyi are four to eight feet thick. Hidden vaulted corridors reduce the weight and amount of materials used in the upper levels, as is also the case at the Sulamani and Gawdawpalin temples. The mortar is made of such strange ingredients[40] as molasses and buffalo hide but it is of excellent quality, as the layer of cement is so thin that there is hardly any space between the bricks for a needle to be inserted. That was apparently the test of a good mason. Legends, which may well be true, tell of King Narathu ordering builders' hands chopped to be off if there was enough space between the bricks for a pin. Indeed, in front of an image inside the temple, there is a circular stone slab supposedly used for this punishment. It has a hollowed trough cut in the shape of a man's arm with a notch across the wrist for a blade to slice through.

Narapatisithu (r. 1173–1210), son of King Narathu, built the Gawdawpalin and Sulamani Temples in the Burmese style. Gawdawpalin, meaning "A Throne of Paying Homage", is believed to have been built by King Narapatisithu as an act of penance after he went blind following an act of disrespect to his ancestors.

Left: *Dhammayangyi Temple, merit of King Narathu.*

Below: *This strange-looking block of stone is reputedly where King Narathu would cut off the hands of builders who failed to meet his stringent construction standards.*

During King Narapatisithu's rule of 37 years, Burmese was close to being made the official language. Only the opening lines of prayers in stone inscriptions of the time were in Mon or Pali; the rest of the text was etched in Burmese. The language was simple, concise and clear, so much so that nearly a thousand years later, in the early twentieth century, young Burmese writers fed up with flowery court-style writings began to adopt a style based on these old inscriptions, beginning the literary era of Khit San Sarpay, or "Dawning of the New Writings".

Many temples have wall paintings, an educational and decorative tradition that later spread to pagodas and temples all over Myanmar. Monks in monastic schools, which still exist in some places, educated children and the country achieved a high literacy rate. Books were expensive so education and the awareness of Buddhist stories were accomplished through the wall paintings. These later evolved into painted panels lining the top of walkways to pagodas.

During King Narapatisithu's reign, Bagan once again enjoyed peace and prosperity. He was succeeded by his son, Nadaungmya, "The King of the Many Earrings", also known as Htilominlo (r. 1210–1234), "Chosen by King and Guardian Spirit of the Royal Umbrella".

The temple he built, also called the Htilominlo, is another fine example of the late Bagan period style temple. However, another of his temples that stands out from the other temples of Bagan is the Mahabodhi, styled after the Vajrsana Temple in Bodh Gaya, India. While not an exact replica, it is very much like a Hindu temple in design. The sloping pyramidal spire is lined with row upon row of seated Buddha images. Underneath the spire is a quadrangular prayer hall with a portico at the western side.

King Htilominlo's son, Kyaswa (r. 1234–1250) started work on, but did not complete, the huge Pyatthat Temple, more commonly known as the Pya Tha Da Temple, not far from the Sulamani. Its red brick walls are unplastered and the upper storey was left incomplete probably because the labourers were not paid well. Kyaswa was known as a philosopher

Opposite: *Gawdawpalin Pagoda, merit of King Narapatisithu.*

Left: *Images of the Buddha set in niches at Mahabodhi Pagoda, Bagan.*

Below: *A mural in Bagan showing three seated figures.*

king, as he was more interested in studying Buddhist texts than in administration. He left all state affairs, presumably including payment for labour, in the hands of his son, the Crown Prince Uzana, who in turn was more interested in sporting with elephants. King Kyaswa even wrote a philosophical thesis for his concubines to learn by heart, which they did with some effort even though they had not the faintest idea of its meaning. He created a lotus-filled lake where wild birds frolicked. By the lake, he built a summer palace. There, he spent his days happily studying Buddhist texts. At the age of 57, while practising with his sword, he pierced himself and so "returned to rest in the abode of celestials".

The unfinished Pya Tha Da Temple, now in ruins, has a 15-square-foot solid core. Parts of its walls have broken away to reveal the construction techniques used to reduce mass and weight in larger temples during the Late Bagan period. One can see the relieving vaults arched over the shrines and corridors, with open space between them.

The barrel vault over the main shrine, facing east, is the largest vault in Bagan, measuring 25 feet wide and 50 feet long.

Pya Tha Da also refers to the two days of a lunar month calculated as most unfortunate, and locals believe it was this inauspicious choice of name that prevented the temple from being completed.

Stone inscriptions found in Bagan recorded the building of other structures apart from temples such as libraries, monasteries and ordination halls. Many monasteries were built of brick and had wooden porches. U Pali Thein is an ordination hall commissioned by a monk named U Pali[41] who lived in the early thirteenth century. It is a rectangular structure with a doorway on each side. Built of brick, it nonetheless followed the usual construction plan for wooden structures. The roof is ridged and there are half pillars and simulated cross beams at each end of the building. The interior wall paintings are believed to be from the eighteenth century.

The other type of religious structure is the cone-shaped stupa, or *zedi*, as it is known in Burmese. In ages past, cosmology and astrology had been the province of Hindu Brahmins in the service of the court, as Buddhism does not cater to such practices or secular rituals. The mythical Mount Meru of Hindu belief was thus translated into Burmese culture as Myintmo Mountain. The stupa with its towering spire is based on this concept of the metaphysical mountain to symbolise a rising force.

Opposite: *Scaffolding surrounds Pya Tha Da Temple in Bagan as it is being restored.*

Below: *U Pali Thein, a brick ordination hall in Bagan commissioned by the Buddhist monk U Pali.*

Opposite: *Buphaya Pagoda on the banks of the Ayeyarwady River. Its name was derived because it is shaped like a* bu, *or gourd.*

Left: *The marvellous gilded form of Shwezigon Pagoda in Bagan dominates a clear blue sky.*

Buddha images cast from precious metals as well as gemstones and jewellery were usually enshrined in the foundations of stupas. Buphaya Pagoda, believed to be one of the earliest pagodas in Bagan[42], has a cylindrical dome much in the shape of the older pagodas of the Pyu era while the Lawkananda has a slightly outward curve towards the bottom edge. The shape of the dome is thus akin to that of a bell, a Burmese form that would become the prototype for all the later stupas constructed in Myanmar.

An incomparably beautiful example of the stupa is the Shwezigon Pagoda. Three receding square terraces form the foundation of this stupa. On this is set an octagonal base, which provides the transition into the bell-shaped, tapering cone. A wide, upright midsection with floral motifs on the shoulder gives way to a multitude of tapering rings ending in a finial. This is topped with a *hti*. The stupa hence has somewhat of a squat shape but still radiates a sense of power.

Near the base of the stupa is a small, cup-sized hollow in the stone floor that is filled with water. King Kyansittha had worshipped at this spot and the mirror of the water's surface allowed him to look with adoration at the spire while in prayer without raising his eyes upwards. Some who have a less romantic turn of mind say the hollow had a more practical purpose: that constructors used it and another one in the exact opposite position to check the plumb of the stupa.

There are four stairways on each of the three terraces with balustrades in the form of sea monsters called Makara. At the corners

are small stupas in the shape of pots, symbols of prosperity. The lions at each corner of the base of the stupa appear to be an angular variation of a mythical Mon creature, the Manoke Thiha, which has the upper body of a human and the double nether parts of a lion. They are guardians that were once said to strike terror in the hearts of invaders.

On the grounds of this famed temple stand 37 *nat* images in a pavilion. Believed to have been placed there by order of King Anawrahta, they are symbols of the superstitious belief that the wise king allowed the baser level of his people to hold. Buddhist philosophy is a hard rule to live by; one is entirely responsible for the salvation of oneself, with no Almighty to pray to for succour. It must relieve the

human mind somewhat to believe that other forces can help in return for offerings of music, food, flowers and drink[43].

The Shwezigon is not the only pagoda to have plaques decorating its corridors or exterior walls. For example, the Petleik Pagodas, believed to have been built by King Anawrahta, have unglazed ceramic plaques. The Shwezigon Pagoda itself has glazed plaques, as do Htilominlo Temple, the Ananda Temple and Dhamayazika Pagoda, built by King Narapatisithu in 1198. The Mingalar Zedi built by King Narathihapate (r. 1256–1287) has more than a thousand such plaques. In 1963, the archaeology department discovered old glazed ceramic kilns in Bagan, including one measuring eight feet at the base and ten feet high. Ceramic experts have found that Bagan glazed ceramic ware are made of silica, white clay, calcium, lead oxide, tin oxide, copper oxide, chrome oxide, vanadium oxide and feldspar[44].

The construction of the Mingalar Zedi, the stupa with more than a thousand plaques, would mark the end of Bagan in the thirteenth century. King Narathihapate's arrogant treatment of emissaries from China, a misunderstanding about the disappearance of a few of the said emissaries and a few other factors brought the wrath of the ruler of China, Kublai Khan, to bear on Bagan at a time when the Khan was eager to expand his empire to encompass all of Asia. The Bagan armies fought valiantly, as recorded in Marco Polo's *Travels*[45] but the king fled southwards, forever earning him the name T'ayoke Pyay Min or the "King who fled from the Chinese". The Khan did not leave anyone of his kind to rule, instead installing a puppet Burmese king. The king was soon overthrown by three princes of Shan-Burmese descent. They moved their capital further north to a place near what was to become the city of Mandalay. The remnants of Burmese nobility escaped to Toungoo, some 200 miles southeast of Bagan, far from the Ayeyarwady and deep in the teak jungles. Toungoo was to rise as a powerful kingdom two centuries later.

Opposite: *The golden statue of a chinthe stands on the grounds of Shwezigon Pagoda in Bagan.*

Left: *Detail of a stucco at Shwezigon Pagoda showing a celestial being.*

ROYAL TRADITIONS

Ratnapura:
City Of Gems

The official title of Inwa (Ava) is Ratnapura, the "City of Gems". The city is a little gem of a lush, fertile island bordered by the Ayeyarwady River, the Myit Nge River and a wide canal. Various kings have alternatively decided to settle here or abandon the place, as it has been the capital five times under the rule of a number of different dynasties.

Traditional Burmese belief holds that the axis of the universe is Myintmo Mountain[46] and that the mountain is surrounded by seven mountain ranges and seven seas. At each of the four cardinal points of the universe is an island, each inhabited by humans. We live on Zapudipar, the southern island, known to modern science as planet Earth. Humans with a better standard of living inhabit the other three islands. They are the fortunate who live up to 500 or a thousand years and know no suffering. Only the humans of the southern island, being the humans on Earth, undergo hardship and pain, not to mention ill health and a shorter life span. It is said that Earthlings gladly bear this suffering because it gives them the will and the chance to pursue and ultimately attain Nirvana.

The exact centre of Zapudipar Island is believed to be the spot where the Thiha Thana Throne[47] is located in Burmese royal palaces. Capital cities and palaces were relocated from time to time and the centre of the earth would have shifted as well, it would seem, to a new spot chosen by the king and his astrologers. The centre of the earth was shifted never more often than at Inwa. Further, since the throne must rest directly under the nine-tiered *pyatthat* roof of Myay Nan, the Great Audience Hall, the palace roof was repeatedly moved as well. *Pyatthat* roofs, significantly the most prominent symbols of Burmese architecture, are used only for religious buildings and palaces.

The British knew Inwa as Ava, the anglicised pronunciation of A-wa. Locals used to refer to the place as "A-wa" before westerners arrived, just as they used to refer to Myanmar as "Miamma". "Inwa" is a name that came into popular use only about 150 years ago. Not far from Inwa, on the bank of the Ayeyarwady, stand the twin pagodas Shwekyet-yet and Shwekyet-kya. People from surrounding villages still come down to the shallow waters near these pagodas to water their cattle, do their laundry and bathe in the cool of the evening.

Inwa was first set up as capital by Thadominbya, a warrior king of Shan and Burmese descent. Successive rulers of Inwa waged war for decades and left no lasting monuments. The early history of Inwa, from its founding in 1364 to its demise in 1555, was therefore a time of war and bloodshed. It was the time of such heroes as Prince Min Ye Kyaw Swa who became a general at the age of 13 and who died in the arms of his Mon enemies after refusing medical care. Both sides, it was recorded, mourned the loss of the warrior prince. There was also the thief Nga Tet Pya who stole from the rich and gave to the poor. When he was finally captured, the rogue dared to ask the king for the hand of his prettiest queen in marriage. The king liked his courage so much that the thief was offered the position of a commander in the royal army although the request to marry the queen was refused. During this time too lived such great queens as Shin Saw Pu[48], who later ruled the Mon kingdom under the Mon name Banya Thau, and the scheming beauty Shin Bo Mai, who married five kings and poisoned the third after only three months of marriage. It speaks of her charms that two kings were not deterred from marrying her after this murder.

In later periods, kings married off their sisters, nieces and daughters to other rulers to strengthen alliances. In spite of the chaotic

battles that raged between the Mon, the Rakhine, the Shan and the Burmese of Inwa and Toungoo for nearly three centuries, the Burmese language, established since the tenth century, attained the height of poetic beauty during this era. New styles of composition emerged. Beautiful poems composed by eminent poets of the era, including those of two women, Mi Nyo of Rakhine and Mi Hpyu of Inwa, are studied to this day. Two scholar-monks, Shin Maha Thila Wuntha and

Shin Maha Rathta Thara, wrote in Burmese instead of the traditional Pali and left great religious epics to posterity. Shin Maha Thila Wuntha also wrote *Yarzawun Kyaw*, "The History of Kings", in 1502. The work is the first accountable historical treatise about Myanmar.

An early sixteenth century inscription left a detailed record of a new palace built by King Narapati in Inwa. Construction began with a ritual of supplication to the spirits on 30 December 1509

with the official occupation occurring on 10 August 1510. Only the ceremonies for each stage of construction and occupation were recorded but examinations of the records found them to be similar to those performed during the building of King Kyansittha's palace in Bagan 408 years earlier[49].

As Inwa declined in power at the onset of the sixteenth century, the strength of the Toungoo Kingdom rose, culminating in the second Burmese empire of King Bayinnaung. By 1752, the kingdom of Inwa had seriously declined and it was conquered by the Mon king Banya Dala. However, a new Burmese dynasty rose to challenge Mon rule. It was led by U Aung Zeya, a prosperous farmer in his thirties who laid siege to Inwa and reclaimed upper Myanmar to found the third Burmese empire in 1753. Forty-six Burmese villages gathered under him. It was said that his mother urged her sons to battle, calling out to them that she would birth more sons if they should fall.

Taking the royal name King Alaungpaya[50] (r. 1752–1760), U Aung Zeya became the founder of the Konbaung dynasty. As the conqueror of Inwa, he had to build a new palace in place of the old one to commemorate his rule of the centre of the Earth. However, as he had neither the desire to live in Inwa nor the time to build a new palace, he merely replaced the nine-tiered *pyatthat* roof of the Great Audience Hall, technically fulfilling the rites of setting up a new palace. He then set up the capital at his hometown of Shwebo. The capital was moved back to Inwa only when his second son, Hsinbyushin (r. 1763–1776), "Lord of the White Elephant", ascended the throne.

Konbaung was to be the last Burmese royal dynasty. A few beautiful buildings from the time of this dynasty remain in Inwa, a place still ringed by a wall in the shape of a crouching lion. A brick passage once traversed by kings meanders through what is now merely a large village.

Pages 54–55: *One of many pagodas located on the shores of the Ayeyarwady River.*

Opposite and left: *Two examples of the statues of Inwa. The one opposite is of an owl while the one on the left is of a* chinthe, *a mythical creature.*

Pages 58–59: *Maha Aung Mye Bonzan Monastery in Inwa, donated in 1819 by Nan Madaw Mai Nu, favourite queen of King Bagyidaw.*

The Maha Aung Mye Bonzan Monastery is noteworthy because it is built of brick but has the architectural features of traditional wooden monasteries. This large building, which took five years to build, is decorated with intricate bas-relief friezes of stylised flora and mythical animals. It was donated in 1819 by Nan Madaw[51] Mai Nu, the favourite queen of Bagyidaw (r. 1819–1837), fifth king in the Konbaung dynasty. He was the last king to set up a capital at Inwa, moving it from Amarapura, where his grandfather, King Bodawpaya (r. 1782–1819), had settled.

Mai Nu was a commoner, the daughter of a prison warden, while Bagyidaw was a king who detested the restrictions of royalty. He preferred to be outdoors on horse or elephant, accompanied by officials who were his childhood friends, and seemed to have been somewhat a Renaissance man, to use a modern term. He had learned monks, Brahmins and scholars compile a chronicle of kings, allowing them to work in the Glass Palace, a pavilion walled with glass mosaic. The treatise became famous as The Glass Palace Chronicles. He also supported the performing arts, especially the marionette stage, which peaked in terms of power[53] and skill during his time.

By King Bagyidaw's reign, foreign traders and missionaries were a common sight in Inwa. One of them noted that the king "was of a playful, affable, and withal a kindly disposition. He was of dark complexion, and in person small and slender. He was mentally incapable of any continuous effort, but his physical activity was remarkable and scarcely a day passed that he did not go on the river, or ride on horseback or on an elephant". His favourite queen, Mai Nu was "without much personal beauty, but of an imperious and commanding nature".

Mai Nu and her elder brother U Oh controlled and abused much of the power in the kingdom. This situation persisted until Crown Prince Tharyarwaddy, the king's younger brother, summarily took over the throne. He promptly executed Mai Nu and U Oh and put the deposed Bagyidaw in luxurious imprisonment.

The Maha Aung Mye Bonzan monastery was not the only legacy Nan Madaw Mai Nu left on her death in 1837; her only daughter and granddaughter were both partly responsible, through their greed for power, for the end of their dynasty and the British conquest of Burma 48 years later.

The only trace remaining of the palace at Inwa is a watchtower. It was damaged by the great earthquake of 1838 and now leans precariously to one side. A wall of teak trunks, once part of a stockade to train wild elephants, stands in splendid isolation. It was a sport much enjoyed by King Bagyidaw, who owned a thousand male elephants. Women did not attend the elephant training sessions, but Mai Nu and the court ladies enjoyed other activities.

Inwa is a fertile and green land, well-irrigated by the rivers and canal ringing it. Brick water tanks store clean drinking water for monasteries or palaces. The borders of such water storage tanks, from smaller ones to reservoirs six miles wide, were enclosed by a low brick wall with stairs and steps as well as archways decorated with stucco designs. One in the palace was used as a place for the royal children to frolic and splash in during the heat of summer.

Above: *This leaning watchtower is all that remains of the palace at Inwa.*

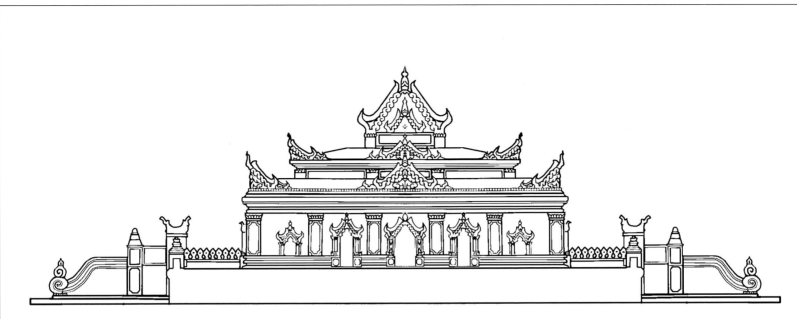

Above: *Maha Aung Mye Bonzan Monastery, also known as Mai Nu's Brick Monastery, Inwa.*

Above: *A cross-section of Maha Aung Mye Bonzan Monastery.*

Right: *Bargaya Monastery in Inwa is famed for the 267 teak pillars that raise the structure off the ground.*

Above: *Detail of a stair balustrade at Bargaya Monastery.*

Above: *Door frame of Bargaya Monastery, Inwa.*

The Bargaya Monastery is built almost completely of teak. Only the the stairs and the caps of the pillars on the patio are made of different materials, the latter being of marble. It is a sprawling building with high patios and cool, dark chambers. Balustrades, doors and railings are decorated with ornate carvings of traditional motifs. Two-hundred-and-sixty-seven columns of teak trunks and 44 beams, also cut from whole logs, hold up the raised floor and low ceilings.

The main pavilion is a small, high-ceilinged chamber set higher than the patio. Two stairways ascend to it. Its five-tiered *pyatthat* roof rises up in receding crests. At the back is a big hall for public ceremonies, connected to the main pavilion by a small chamber called the *sanu* hall, where guest monks are received.

The weatherworn monastery stands in lonely splendour in the middle of wide paddy fields with palm and banana trees and thorny green bushes clustered around its shady base. Gentle tendrils of wild vines climb over the doors where celestial doorkeepers stand in high relief. They gaze impassively upon the empty dustiness beyond, just as they had once looked upon kings and their royal retinue.

In another empty field, the beautiful shell of the ruined Lay Htut Gyi Temple, destroyed in the earthquake of 1838, stands alone on a mound of its own bricks. Wild flowers grow thickly in its cracks and small butterflies flit delicately around the fierce faces of stone ogres fallen and decayed. Designed after the Ananda of Bagan, traces of its majestic elegance can still be seen in the high doorway in each of the four façades, panels set with figures of the King of the Celestials and mythical creatures of stucco cavorting along the walls.

In 1783, the capital was moved again from Inwa to Amarapura. During these restless times rife with uprisings fomented by usurpers, invasions into the Rakhine and Siamese kingdoms and dealings with the French and English, another renaissance of arts and literature emerged. Plays, songs and dances from this period are still popular to this day.

Surely no other city in Myanmar has seen as much strife and unrest. Now Inwa is a wide expanse of lush paddy fields dotted with shady groves of tamarind trees. Mingalar T'dar, "The Most Auspicious Gateway", and many parts of the city wall still stand, guarding a place that at long last is at peace.

Left: *A carved wooden balustrade decorated with traditional motifs at Bargaya Monastery, Inwa. Note the marble capstone on the pillar.*

Amarapura:
City of Immortality

King Bodawpaya (r. 1782–1819), who founded Amarapura in 1783, left a strange monument not in Amarapura but at a place called Mingun on the western bank of the Ayeyarwady River. It was a temple he planned to build to a height of 500 feet but which he left unfinished at 160 feet due to omens that circulated foretelling the downfall of the dynasty upon its completion. The foundation measures 450 feet on each side of its square foundation. A 90-tonne bell hangs in a pavilion nearby. It was cast in the hope of gracing the Mingun Pagoda platform and remains the biggest hanging bell in the world, next to the world's biggest brick pile. A witty and wise minister in King Bodawpaya's cabinet, U Paw Oo, could often persuade the king from other foolhardy projects but apparently not this one[53].

In Amarapura, only the remains of the Treasury and the Record Office buildings can be seen today out of the many palace buildings that once graced this wide area.

In 1795, British envoy Michael Symes arrived at Amarapura, which he confused with Inwa, and gave a detailed account of his experiences. He attended one of the morning sessions of audience in the *Hluttaw*, or "Lotoo" as he heard and spelled it, but unfortunately the king, Bodawpaya, failed to attend. Symes noted the arrival of the Crown Prince "Engy Teekien"[54] borne on an open palanquin and shaded by a large gold fan. Officials and Brahmins arrived in order, dressed in their robes of white, red and blue, and gold insignia. Their servants followed, carrying water flagons and betel boxes, some of a size that to Symes looked "no inconsiderable load for a man". It was a show of prestige and rank to have a bigger-sized betel box than others. Some of them were even fashioned of gold and had rubies set in the lid. The officials were not about to lose an ounce of prestige, exhibited by the size of their utensils, however cumbersome they might be. "In every part of this ostentatious parade, perfect regularity was maintained," Symes wrote. Elephants and horses also featured in the procession that would take place every morning of the working week[55].

Above: *Image of a* nat, *who is also an ogre (note the headdress), Amarapura.*

Opposite: *The bright white structure of the prototype for the Mingun Pagoda, left unfinished, at Amarapura.*

After waiting two hours for this parade to end, he entered the hall of the *Hluttaw*. He wrote that "a stranger cannot fail to be surprised at the magnificence of its appearance; it is supported by 77 pillars, disposed in 11 rows, each consisting of seven. The roof of the building is composed of distinct stages, the highest in the centre. The row of pillars that supported the middle, or most lofty roof, we judge to be 35 or 40 feet in height; the others gradually diminish as they approach the extremities of the building, and those which sustain the balcony are not more than 12 or 14 feet. At the farther part of the hall there is a high gilded lattice, extending quite across the building, and in the centre of the lattice is a gilded door, which, when opened, displays the throne; this door is elevated five or six feet from the floor, so that the throne must be ascended by means of steps at the back, which are not visible, nor is the seat of the throne to be seen, except when the king comes in person to the throne. At the bottom of the lattice there is a gilt balustrade, three or four feet high, in which umbrellas and several other insignia of state were displayed".

The crown prince sat on a small stool but others sat on mats, Symes most uncomfortably trying to tuck his legs under him. The ceremony of presenting letters from the Governor General of India and answering courteous inquiries went on as if the king had been present[56]. To the king's polite inquiries after the British king and family and the state and prosperity of Britain, Symes as courteously replied that Britain enjoyed perfect tranquillity in spite of enmity with France and the state of war in Europe. Thus the "audience" ended and Symes and his companions were served about a hundred small dishes of sweets and savouries, a few of which he tasted and found "very palatable".

All traces of the palace have disappeared. Only the tombs of the two kings, Bodawpaya and Bagyidaw, strange and fascinating men both, remain. However, beautiful temples are still standing. Patodawgyi Pagoda, with its marble carvings of scenes from the life of Buddha, is situated near the banks of the man-made Taungthaman Lake.

A mile-long wooden bridge connects the shores of Taungthaman Lake. Known as U Bein's Bridge, it was built by a junior official during the reign of King Bagan (r. 1846–1853). He used whole trunks of teak from a discarded palace of Inwa to build this wide and picturesque bridge. At the banks on one end of the bridge stands the Kyautaw Gyi

Above: *The famed Mingun Bell in Mingun, the largest hanging bell in the world.*

Opposite: *The Mingun Pagoda in Amarapura, damaged by earthquake in 1838.*

Pagoda, "The Great Stone", so called because it has a huge image of the Buddha hewn from a single block of marble. The porch walls are covered with paintings of various pagodas from all over Myanmar as well as religious scenes and depictions of the daily lives of villagers.

The Nagayon Pagoda, "The Embraced by the Dragon Pagoda", at Amarapura is different from other temples of the same name elsewhere, for the dragon here embraces the entire building and not just the image inside. This strange temple astounded Henry Yule who saw it in 1855. He wrote that when "seen from a distance it perplexed us much... in some points of view it appeared as a pagoda; in others as one of the gigantic lions or griffins.... coming nearer we found it to be both one and the other... the lower part was a temple... encased as it were in the bowels of the gigantic monster, whose elevated jaws and scaly crest formed a spire over it".

Left: *The strangely-shaped Nagayon Pagoda, Amarapura.*

Below: *The interior of Kyautaw Gyi Pagoda, Amarapura.*

Opposite: *Detail of the sculpted balustrade at Patodawgyi Pagoda, Amarapura.*

Pages 72-73: *U Bein's Bridge, a wooden bridge that is still in use more than a century after it was constructed.*

Despite its titular claim to immortality, Amarapura was the capital for only a few short years. Climatic forces, astrological calculations, portentious dreams and whispered omens resulted in the decision of the second-last king of Burma to relocate the capital just a few miles away to the foot of Mandalay Hill in 1856. The two cities of Amarapura and Mandalay have since grown and merged. Today in Amarapura, in place of the sounds of royal pomp and ceremony, one would hear the steady rhythms of craftsmen busy in their small workshops: casters of bronze, carvers of wood and ivory and beaters of gold. At present, Amarapura enjoys the glory of being the seat of the best craftsmen in the country, a distinction decidedly more stable than that of being the seat of royalty.

Yadanabon:
City of the Mound of Gems

Yadanabon, or Mandalay as it came to be called due to its proximity to Mandalay Hill, was the last of the royal capitals. It was built by King Mindon (r.1853-1878) who was unhappy to be living in Amarapura. The probable reasons for this unhappiness, not recorded in historical chronicles, may be that Amarapura as a capital had seen its king losing lower Burma to the British in the Anglo-Burmese wars of 1824 and 1852. Furthermore, when the British envoy Sir Arthur Phayre came in 1855, he sailed his gunboat right into Taungthaman Lake and moored

Below: *The intricately carved roofs of the Royal Palace in Mandalay.*

Opposite: *A view of the compound of the Royal Palace from the palace watchtower. Most of the buildings are replicas, except the white brick building, which is an original structure.*

not far from the palace, almost looming over its sacred spires. These were reasons enough for King Mindon to abandon Amarapura.

An early-twentieth-century book compiled from old manuscripts, *The Building of the City of Mandalay as the Throne City*[57], recorded in detail the plans for moving the capital from Amarapura. It noted earthquakes and fallen shrines and recorded the minutes of meetings attended by the king, the clergy and the cabinet. It was also recorded that various petitions flew from the styli of learned men arguing for or against the move. Court astrologers worked their calculations and wise men submitted treatises to interpret omens. A council of 24 Abbots even sternly admonished that "this Royal habit of relocating the capital now here and now there was placing a great strain on all creatures, monk and men, and animals, horses, cows, oxen, dogs, cats, not to mention the loss of lives of turtles and fish and shrimp in the abandoned moats".

King Mindon himself said little but finally disclosed that he had had three wondrous dreams full of good portent for the move. None could argue against the dreams and the matter was settled. Anyone who wished to remain in Amarapura was free to do so but in the end few did. Nothing in the king's dreams foretold the occupation of his new capital by foreign forces a mere 25 years later, the exile of his son or the end of his dynasty.

The land at the foot of Mandalay Hill was cleared on an auspicious day in February 1857 by men selected for their auspicious day of birth. A few days later, the ceremony to mark out the palace site was held. According to the book on the building of Mandalay: "First, while facing east, homage was paid to the Three Gems[58] and the lesser gods.

Then eight pairs of matched oxen without any defects, adorned with bridles of gold and silver, were yoked to ploughs of gold and silver, these driven by eight men of goodly birthdays[59]. Then eight Brahmins of pure descent led eight sons of wealthy men, each with a spade of gold or silver and facing east, they turned clockwise in pacing out the lengths of the city and the palace"[60].

Several days later, a clearing nearby was also marked out so that a temporary palace could be constructed to be used on inspection trips while the city was being built. Timber used was from trees found on land of "purity", meaning such land as was not near cemeteries, foul smelling places or the like. Tree trunks were checked for blemishes and knots, and chosen because they stood straight.

The construction of Mandalay City lasted from 1857 to 1861. King Mindon also took great care planning the city outside Nan Myo, the walls of the capital city. The streets ran straight and wide, crossing perpendicular to each other. He built canals to bring water to the city and 20 parks to retain some coolness on this hot plain.

Originally, there were 54 *yut kwet*, or wards, in the city; seven on the east, 13 to the south, 29 to the west and five to the north. Most were given such grandiose titles as Pyi Gyi Kyet Thayay, "Auspiciousness of the Great Nation"; Yan Myo Lon, "Secure from All Harm"; and Palai Ngwe Yaung, "Silvery Pearl Colour". Some were known by the work done in the area: wards or streets of knife-makers, bamboo-sellers, goldleaf-beaters, embroiderers and such. A section named Pyi Gyi Pyaw Bwai, "Joy of the Great Nation", was set apart for brothels[61]. The choice of name is not surprising as prostitutes are known in polite terms as *Meinma Shwin,* "Joyful Women".

Certainly, far more care was taken in building the palace. It was recorded that every single act of labour such as the sawing of timber or the sharpening of nails had to be done using gilded tools at auspicious times and days. More important tasks required ministers and officials to lead certain ceremonies which were performed at a precise and carefully-chosen moment.

The palace wall was surrounded by a wide moat. Each side of the wall was, according to Burmese units of measurement, 600 *ta* long, or a little more than a-mile-and-a-quarter long. Altogether, the wall was 2,400 *ta* long, a figure also representative of the year it was according to the Buddhist era. There were 12 gates in the city wall to symbolise the 12 months, each gate roofed with a seven-tiered *pyatthat*. Along the wall were 48 pavilions for the 48 weeks in a year. Four bridges at each compass point crossed over the moat. The moat was fed with river water through a series of dams and canals. Until the 1980s, it provided the town with a sufficient supply of water.

Four glazed jars were also buried in the four corners of the wall, each jar being "filled with 120 viss[62] of a mixture of oils, sesame and mustard, then tightly covered and buried on the thirteenth day of the Waxing Moon Month of Kason, precisely at two strokes by the clock early on Sunday morning". The items buried in the foundations of wall, moat and palace as tokens of prosperity numbered in the hundreds.

They included runes, charms, flasks of rose water, packets of the Nine Noble Gems[63] and coils of thread spun by "three virgin daughters of princes, three virgin daughters of Brahmins and three virgin daughters of wealthy men".

Although local records do not mention human sacrifices in the building of the city walls, it may be assumed that this ritual could not have been ignored. King Mindon was a deeply religious man and at times when he had no wish to be responsible for a sinful decision, he would pretend not to hear the question put to him. Unpleasant news had to be reported to him only during the time he sat on the royal toilet in the mornings, as the place was considered already inauspicious. If, for example, he wanted to pardon a condemned prisoner, he would say so. Otherwise, he would remain silent, and thus would technically be free of the sin of killing. If he had no wish to be part of the act of burying people alive under his city gates, it could have been done under the orders of Brahmin astrologers. Whether human sacrifices actually occurred would have depended not on the king's decision but on the amount of power court astrologers wielded at the time[64].

Below: *Detail of woodcarvings used in the recreation of the Royal Palace, Mandalay.*

Opposite: *A gate and the wall that surrounds the Royal Palace.*

Left: *The Royal Palace moat in Mandalay with fortifications in the background.*

The 239 dwellings inside the walls of the city but outside the palace proper included several homes for the aged, the dowager queens' apartments, residences of officials, barracks and even a place for "Retired Nanny Mi Lay Win".

Never were architectural traditions as strictly adhered to as in the building of the palace. It was built to incorporate a total of 360 teak pillars to symbolise the 360 days of the lunar calendar. The number of levels in any *pyatthat* tiered roof had to be odd but could not be the same as that of a palace, monastery or pagoda pavilion. The Great Audience Hall had a nine-tiered roof, directly under which was placed the Lion Throne. Other audience rooms for different occasions were set up at their proper places with corresponding thrones.

King Mindon built many pagodas and temples within the city, believing that the Buddha himself had once stood on Mandalay Hill and pointed out to the land below as where a city of great importance to Buddhism would one day flourish. In 1859, on the "Twelfth Waxing Day of the Wagaung Moon Month", King Mindon entered Mandalay with due pomp and ceremony. Marching with him were rows of infantry, cavalry, officials, ministers, ladies, musicians, dancers, Brahmins and learned men. They held their white and gold umbrellas aloft, banners and insignia flashing in the sunlight, as even elephants and horses paced solemnly to the beat of the Big Royal Drum. The procession walked on pathways covered in white sand and bordered with diamond-shaped latticed fences of bamboo known as *Yaza Mat Kwet,* "Squares of Royalty"[65]. Banana and sugarcane plants set up at intervals for their green foliage added freshness to the scene. Kneeling commoners lined the route, paying obeisance with heads bowed and hands clasped.

Among King Mindon's many merits is the Kuthodaw Pagoda. Here, the complete Buddhist texts may be found, incised onto 729 marble slabs, each one housed in its own pavilion. The pagoda was built in 1857 to commemorate and set in stone the Buddhists texts revised from the Fifth Buddhist Synod, which King Mindon had held from 1860 to 1868[66].

A year before his death in 1878, King Mindon discovered an immense marble block from the Sagyin quarry[67]. He had an image carved out of it, and painted in the eyes himself to "open the glorious face". It is inside the Kyauktaw Gyi Pagoda near Mandalay Hill.

Above: *Myay Nan, The Great Audience Hall of the Royal Palace in Mandalay.*
Opposite: *Pavillions in the compound of the Kuthodaw Pagoda, Mandalay.*

King Mindon's rule of 25 years was prosperous and peaceful overall. However, not all was well within his family. His nominated heir was the popular and intelligent Prince Kanaung, younger brother to King Mindon, who had adhered to his ancestor Alaungpaya's decree that brothers succeed and not sons. Unwilling to be passed over, two of King Mindon's sons had assassinated the Crown Prince and fled south to find sanctuary with the British.

Prince Kanaung had been a forward-looking and modern individual, keen to upgrade the military as he already saw the westerners' greed. He had tried to improve his stock of arms and munitions but any advancement to his plans were terminated by the words of the king's abbot[68]. King Mindon dared not name anyone heir, and the matter was left unresolved as he lay dying.

It gave the Queen of the Middle Palace, Hsin Hpyu Ma Shin, daughter of the infamous Mai Nu, a chance to propose a candidate in 20-year-old Prince Thibaw, her daughter's sweetheart. She had no sons and there were no other senior queens left to challenge her power. She kept everyone away from the dying king and on his death declared that King Mindon had agreed to her choice. To be safe, as soon as the king passed to the realm of celestials, Hsin Hpyu Ma Shin imprisoned and later murdered many of King Mindon's other sons, not a few of them older and more able, including Prince Mekera and Prince Thonze[69].

Both Hsin Hpyu Ma Shin and her middle daughter, Supayalat, were obsessed with being Chief Queen, the Queen of the Southern Palace[70], as it did not satisfy them enough to be one of the four senior queens. King Mindon had refused to elevate Hsin Hpyu Ma Shin to the palace when his Chief Queen, Queen Sanda Dewi, a well-loved and wise lady, passed away. Scholars believe this fact had a lot to do with Supayalat's obsession.

Thibaw was a mild-mannered, scholarly young man and his supporters thought he could be easily manipulated. They also planned to make Hsin Hpyu Ma Shin's obedient eldest daughter, Supayagyi, Chief Queen. This gentle but none-too-pretty princess had been Thibaw's first sweetheart. The younger and prettier Supayalat, keenly aware of future events, had snatched him away for herself when the prince, at 18 years of age, came into his father's favour after passing the highest religious exam with flying colours.

By tradition, Supayalat, the younger sister, should have allowed Supayagyi to become Chief Queen if both married the king, who was also their half-brother. However, at the precise moment in the coronation ceremony, Supayalat had pushed her way into her sister's place to be anointed Chief Queen. The humiliated Supayagyi retired to her mother's apartments and remained a virgin queen[71]. The dowager queen's hopes of becoming the power behind the throne collapsed at the same moment.

Opposite: *King Mindon's grave in Mandalay.*

Above: *A mural at Kyautaw Gyi Pagoda, Amarapura.*

The dowager mother and queen daughter replaced the officials at court with those who pleased them most. Together with Kinwun Mingyi U Kaung and Taing Dar Mingyi U Hpoe, the most powerful ministers in the royal court, they were too busy manipulating the king to recognise the danger posed by the British and the French. Both nations were eyeing the riches of Burma, which, besides teak, included the ruby mines at Mogok, a place so rich in the gems that it was once said lucky residents turned up flawless stones while digging in their gardens.

In this chaotic time, there were no princes able enough, indeed there were no princes left, to look after the affairs of state. Thibaw, a quiet-natured man, did not even want to be king. He wanted to be left alone with his books and later, the company of a 15-year-old handmaiden he had fallen in love with[72]. Sadly, he had the misfortune of being a king with the wrong type of queen.

When the British sailed up the Ayeyarwady on a fateful November day in 1885 on their final leg of annexation, they dressed up a Burmese clerk in royal robes and had him sit in the prow. They had spread rumours beforehand that they were bringing one of King Mindon's older sons, the exiled Prince Nyaung Yan, to take King Thibaw's place. The gullible Burmese thought they would still retain a Burmese king, and an able one too, if they submitted to the British. They could not have known that Prince Nyaung Yan had passed away of a fever a few weeks prior to this supposed "coronation".

King Thibaw too, it is said, did not want more bloodshed so he had sent orders under the signature of his minister, Kinwun Mingyi U Kaung, not to resist the British. However, some believe King Thibaw had no hand in the surrender and that it was Kinwun Mingyi U Kaung's order that turned Burma over to the British. That U Kaung continued to be of service to the British after the king was exiled earned him the infamy of being a turncoat.

Some historians consider U Kaung a realistic diplomat; others believe he sold out to the British. The argument continues to this day. However, none can deny U Kaung's abilities. He had led the first Burmese mission to Britain, France and Italy in 1872, during which time he kept a diary that has been published and reprinted several times and is still read today[73].

King Thibaw, the heavily-pregnant Supayalat, their two baby daughters and Supayalat's youngest sister, Supayalay[74], were all exiled to a small seaport town in India. The dowager and Supayagyi were sent to Mawlamyine in lower Burma. King Thibaw and Supayalay passed away in India. Supayalat returned to Yangôn in 1919, three years after King Thibaw's death at the age of 59. From that time on, she wore full white. She did so not out of mourning for her late king, she said, but as a symbol of her repentance and regret. She passed away in 1925 at the age of 66.

Following the British occupation in 1885, the palace pavilions were turned into offices and clubs. The sound of western boots clumping on wooden floors invaded what had once been the home of royalty. The British themselves fled the premises during World War II in the face of the Japanese invasion. None of the timber pavilions in the palace survived the ravages of fire and bombs during the war[75].

The only pavilion that remains is the one in which King Mindon passed away, a wooden pavilion once set to the north of the Glass Palace. King Thibaw had moved the structure out of the palace walls and donated it to be used as a monastic building. The Shwe Kyaung Daw, "The Golden Palace Monastery" as King Mindon's pavilion came to be known, is an exquisitely carved timber pavilion once completely gilded in gold. Time and the elements have left the wood mostly bare today although the ceiling and some of the pillars deep in the interior are still thickly coated with the original gold leaf.

The pavilion has 150 pillars that are connected at the top by filigreed wooden arches called "bats' wings". The floor is held up by 54 figures of a mythical, serpent-like animal, implying that a royal building such as this was not set on mere ground, but was lifted to the heavens by magical creatures. To protect these wooden figures from damp, stone slabs were placed between them and the bare ground. Celestial beings carved on the doors guard the pavilion from danger. One can even see some European winged angels among them, helping out their Asian cousins. Stylised coils of vines and lotus edge the window and doorframes. The pavilion can be seen today near two of King Mindon's merits, the Kuthodaw Pagoda and the Atu Ma Shi Kyaung.

The Atu Ma Shi Kyaung, "The Incomparable Monastery", was a beautiful brick-based wooden building constructed in 1857. A great image moulded out of King Mindon's lacquered clothes[76] was once enshrined there. The large diamond set in its forehead was stolen by British soldiers after the annexation of upper Burma. The entire monastery, except the brick platform and stairways, was subsequently destroyed by bombs in World War II[77].

One of the undamaged buildings is a monastery King Mindon donated in 1860 to the Abbot U Zar Gara, founder of the austere Shwegyin sect. The monastery lies north of Mandalay Hill and is called the Shwegyin Kyaung. Built entirely of teak, it once had 262 pillars of whole logs supporting its four pavilions. It was recorded that King Mindon paid Master Carpenter U Soe 222,355 pieces of peacock silver Kyat coins for its construction.

Another building that survived the war is the most revered pagoda in Myanmar after the Shwedagon in Yangôn, the Mahamuni Pagoda in Mandalay. It houses the Mahamuni Buddha image, carried over the Rakhine Ranges when King Bodawpaya's son invaded Mrauk U in 1784. The image, apart from the face, has been gold-leafed so thickly that the torso and limbs have lost their shape.

The Shan, Wa and Kokaung living in the northwest frontiers of Myanmar had closer ties with China, being separated from central Myanmar by ridge upon ridge of mountains. Most could trace their ancestry to China, which for some was just across a stream. In many cases, the border would cut through a villager's hut or field. These ethnic Burmese peoples spoke and wrote Chinese instead of Burmese, and when they migrated deeper into Myanmar, most settled in Mandalay. Having suffered poverty for decades, they knew only too well the need for prosperity. The more laid-back and economically non-aggressive Burmese sold off their valuable lands and moved to the suburbs. As a result, just as Yangôn during the early days of British occupation had the look of an Indian town, downtown Mandalay now looks Chinese. However, despite this Sino-Myanmar infusion, Mandalay does retain the elegance and charm of a traditional Burmese city.

After the British colonised Burma and the last king was sent into exile, the glory of Mandalay faded. It is now a bustling business centre with many of its landmarks forever gone. The Zegyo Market, for example, famed for its diverse local goods and sweet-talking sales girls, has been demolished to make way for a high-rise shopping centre. Nonetheless, even with the loss of its buildings, the very name "Mandalay" still evokes strong nostalgia.

Opposite: Atu Ma Shi Kyaung, also known as "The Incomparable Monastery", located in Mandalay.

Right: *Sundown along a riverbank near Mandalay.*

VERNACULAR ARCHITECTURE

Although the last Burmese royal dynasty met its end in 1885, the country has remained locked in rigid tradition, in both the secular and the religious realms. To this day, many conservatives believe that a breach of such rules would cause the King of Celestial Beings to strike down transgressors with a lightning bolt. In days past, the same transgressors would have been chastised not by the King of Celestial Beings but by the kings of the Centre of the Earth, for a breach of the traditions governing secular architecture would have been considered a felony bordering on treason.

Myanmar is bound up in traditions and rituals, so much so that creativity is sometimes stifled to uphold the old ways. One aspect of tradition relating to creativity is that art, masonry and even blacksmithing belong to the *Pan Hsai Myo*, "The Ten Flowers of the Arts"[78].

Architecture was not considered one of the ten but rather a combination of several of the arts. It was governed by its own restrictions in design, plan and decoration, defined according to rank and social status. These restrictions applied to the design and look of palaces, monasteries and homes, right down to the appearance of a prostitute's house[79]. Examples of such ancient secular dwellings no longer exist and the design of later buildings have changed according to time. Only monasteries still exhibit some vestige of the old traditions.

Secular Traditions

The house of a commoner in the time of the kings could be differentiated at a glance from that owned by one who was of noble blood or in government service. Farmers' houses are still commonly set up on a raised platform, as one could stay cool below the structure on hot days[80]. Martaban jars to store oil and pickled fish, or rainwater are half-buried below the house. For royalty, nobles or the wealthy, a high platform meant living above and away from pedestrians and traffic. It also provided an easy way to dismount from an elephant.

Astrologers would be consulted during the construction of a home to determine an auspicious time for the central pillar to be set up, even if the home were just a bamboo hut. The southern pillar of a house, called the *thabye taing,* is the most important. Pillars were usually made from whole tree trunks, chosen with care to ensure that they were of a nice shape and blemish-free. Those that were thick in the middle or at the top were discarded as only trunks with a bigger base, or which were straight, were preferred.

Astrologers also had to make sure that earth ogres did not live at the site of the new building. If ogres were present, monks would be invited to chant mantras vigorously at the site to drive them out. Big trees, especially the *nyaung* tree (*Ficus religiosa*), were seldom cut down, for it was said that Yoke Ka So, Guardian Nat of the Tree, would then be robbed of his dwelling. This *nat* is considered to have the best nature, being ever-willing to help people in distress. Often, small empty wooden houses would be attached to large trees so that people might place flowers or water inside as offerings to Yoke Ka So.

Buildings were thus usually planned around big trees in the garden. In some cases, the walls would be built around a trunk to accommodate a tree. If any large tree had to be removed, the spirits had to be placated with prayers and offerings, and suggestions for alternative accommodations in other trees. An official order from the authorities also had to be read out to Yoke Ka So to at least clear the lumbermen of any blame for cutting down the tree.

Upon the completion of the house, a ritual of cleansing is performed with *thanakha* paste[81] sprinkled from a sprig of *thabye* leaves (*Eugenia jambolana linn*) to make sure that no demons remain. A family never moves into a new house on a Saturday as it symbolises fire, or in the afternoon, which is a "putrid" time of day, and never during the time of the three-month Lent from approximately mid-July to mid-October. Among the first things to be brought into the house would be the Buddhist shrine, the rice pot and the water pot.

Pages 88–89: Detail of the intricate woodcarvings on the roof of *Shwenandaw Monastery in Mandalay*

Right: *The exterior view of a niché, in a house near Pyay, used for the Buddhist Shrine.*

Far right: *An elaborately crafted image of a* nat *in Yangôn.*

Few examples of the ancient Burmese house remain although architectural plans have been drawn up by modern scholars[82]. One plan is for the house that belonged to Kinwun Mingyi U Kaung, built in the town of Ahlone when he was the governor there around 1862. Due to his rank, he was allowed to have certain architectural designs incorporated into his house. A wealthy family bought the house in 1894 and moved it to Monyway Village. They made some changes to the floor plan but it remained a rare example of a house from that period until it burnt down in the 1980s.

The house, made up of a complex of pavilions set on a high patio, was constructed according to strict traditions, except for the fact that builders used metal hinges in the building. As a rule, nails or metal pats were avoided as much as possible. Traditionally, the skill of a builder was judged by the sound emitted when a door flap, attached to the doorframes with mortise joints instead of metal hinges, was opened. The squeak would be evaluated according to how pleasant it was to the ear and which voice, male or female[83], it apparently had.

An official in service to the king, such as Kinwun Mingyi U Kaung, was allowed certain privileges in the architecture of his house, which no one else, not even the very wealthy, could enjoy. He would be allowed to have decorated windows, doorframes and shutters as well as spindled posts for the staircase. Even then, only floral motifs could be used; mythical creatures were strictly for religious decoration. The homes of the privileged could have stairs leading straight towards the front entrance. Monasteries or houses of people without rank or royal blood had to use stairs set parallel to the front wall.

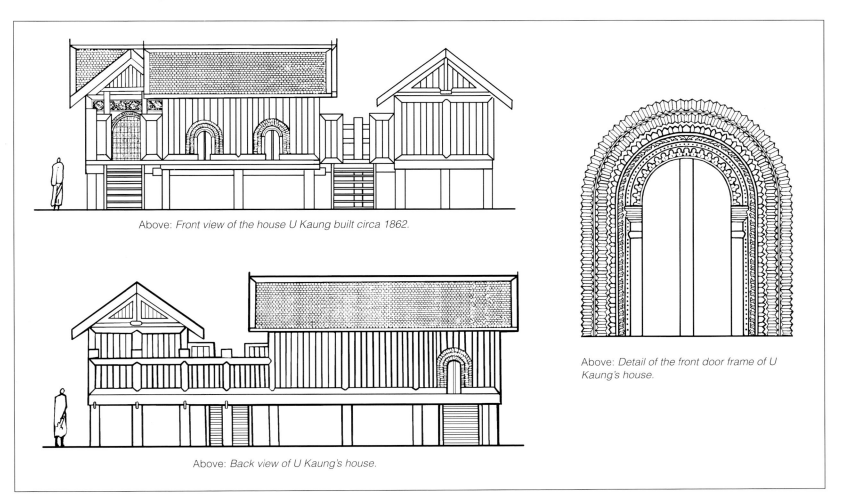

Above: *Front view of the house U Kaung built circa 1862.*

Above: *Back view of U Kaung's house.*

Above: *Detail of the front door frame of U Kaung's house.*

The room at the very front of a house where guests were entertained was called "the show-watching chamber". From this pavilion, a family paying for public entertainment as an act of merit could watch the show in comfort as the stage would be set across from the house in the street. The master bedroom would be in the centre of the whole plan, as the main throne would be in a palace. A family room and kitchen would be located at the back or on the western side. It was assumed that the family room also served as a dining room. The Burmese dining table is low and circular and is literally rolled out at mealtimes. At the back of the house, next to a bedroom, would be the maternity chamber, a necessary part of every residence of affluence. This room had no windows, only a small door through which no men were allowed to pass. The traditional Burmese layout for a house, with several pavilions set on an open patio, has been discarded since colonial times as a more confined plan makes for better security[84].

The typical lower-middle-class Burmese house from the turn of the century has a simpler plan, which is still followed. The house would be set up on stilts and the roof would usually be made of *theke* grass (*Imperata cylindrica*) or, if the house were in the Ayeyarwady delta, the long leaves of the *dhani* palm (*Nipa frutican*). Fronds would be folded over a strip of bamboo rod and secured with a stick. Several of these fabrications would then be placed overlapping one another on a frame of bamboo.

An open veranda would run along the front wall of the house with a stair leading up to it from the side. A pot of cool water with a dipper for visitors and sheaves of paddy hung out for birds might be placed at the far end of the veranda. Visitors would leave their footwear at the front veranda, also called the "shoe-taking-off" place, before stepping into the interior, the floor of which is a hand's span higher than the floor for the veranda.

The whole front wall would be of folding doors. A latticed panel above allowed the air to circulate at night when the doors were shuttered. The floors of each room would be made of smooth planks, shiny with wax polish or daily rubdowns with a wet rag. A smooth rush mat edged with red velvet or cotton would be spread on the floor for visitors, and at meal times, a low round table would be rolled out onto the mat. To welcome guests, a betel box or cheroot tray would be permanently set out on the mat. For added hospitality, a pot of green tea and a dish of pickled tea with condiments would be served.

At either the eastern or southern end of the front room would be the household shrine, complete with its own tiered roof on the outside, set high up against a wall or in a niche built into the wall. A green coconut tied with a strip of red and white cotton might hang in a cane holder set lower than the Buddha shrine for the Household Nat, Min Mahagiri. As he had been burnt to death during the Pyu era, he prefers to dwell in the liquid-filled green coconut. The beds or sleeping mats would have their headboards in the same direction as the shrine, as no one sat or slept with his or her legs pointed towards it. Honoured male guests or the male head of the household would sit or sleep under the shrine while others had to do so slightly to the side of or facing the shrine.

Behind the front room would be bedrooms on either side. A small corridor running between the bedrooms led to the dining room and kitchen in the back of the house. In the kitchen, a glazed jar stored water and wide-slatted floors allowed dishwater to drain away. A few steps away from the kitchen door might be a Martaban jar placed on a large wooden or stone platform, an area which served as the family bathroom. Women bathing in the open air or even by the river managed to be decorously clothed from their armpits down to their ankles. With many family members living in one house, privacy was gained through behaviour rather than walls.

Further away at the far end of the yard would be the toilet. The front yard was usually smaller than the back and would be filled with flowers and bushes planted haphazardly. A bamboo bench would very likely be set out in front for the family to sit on in the evenings or for friends who casually dropped by all day long.

If the building were double-storeyed, the upper floor would have one corner walled off as a room for the parents or for the storage of trunks and, during the day, bedding. Bedding was laid out every night and packed away in the morning, a practice that survives to this day. In the mind of the traditional Burmese, an unmade bed is an inauspicious thing. If the bed were to be removed altogether, so much the better.

Opposite, left: *A water pot amidst the plants in the garden of a home in Yangôn.*

Opposite, right: Pyatthat *roofs on a spirit house in Yangôn.*

Left: *A fountain in the garden of the private residence of Patrick Robert, Yangôn.*

The more affluent lived in timber houses of teak (*Tectona grandis*) or *pyin gadoe* (*Xylia dolabriformis*), both hardwoods that termites cannot damage. Wooden houses are usually coated repeatedly with the dregs of crude oil, which renders them weatherproof. Unfortunately, it also makes them highly flammable. Hence, two tall bamboo poles would be stacked against houses at all times: one with a hook at its tip to pull down burning thatch, and the other with a flat piece of sheet metal to beat out flames.

Until Burma came under British rule, few, if any, of her people had thought to build residences of brick; wood and bamboo being materials that were convenient to use in construction with regard to cost and comfort. Although none of the early timber houses remain intact, some examples of traditional architecture do remain in most small towns and villages.

In current times, most people of comfortable means plan their houses based on more complex and convenient designs that include separate bedrooms with attached bathrooms and modern kitchens.

There is some indifference when it comes to interior decoration for middle-class households, partly because of the close ties that exist in the extended family. Even grown and married children with their own offspring live with their parents. A house is therefore a home in the sense of family relationships but by the same stroke, it becomes impractical to concentrate too much on interior decoration. A Myanmar finds comfort in surroundings he has known for decades, which often means a well-worn home. Comfort in habitat and good food is considered more meaningful. Beauty is expressed more through clothes and jewellery and prestige shown in how much one donates to religion. It is enough that the home is neat and free of dust. Framed pictures of ancestors would be the only decorations on the walls apart from a colourful calendar or two. The only place certain to be prettied up is the Buddha shrine, set in a high niche or in a separate room of its own. Even the poorest family would try to have a fresh vase of leaves or flowers adorning the shrine.

The more affluent sections of Myanmar society, especially the urban wealthy who since the colonial era have sent their children abroad to study, place greater importance on interior decoration. Their homes would probably be decorated with a Myanmar touch, such as the use of antique silver bowls as vases, oil portraits of ancestors and imported carpets and furnishings.

The newly emergent business class displays not only antiques but a variety of folk art and religious artefacts as decorations in their residences, something never before seen in Myanmar. One example is Mangosteen Mansion, a double-storeyed house with two long wings on the ground floor filled with Myanmar artefacts. A village girl would be amazed that her water pot and coconut-shell ladle should find a place in the garden of this mansion.

Opposite, clockwise from top left: *A Karen house, a Burmese house and a Putao house, the last located near the Tibetan border. All have woven walls and are examples of traditionally-styled homes.*

Left: *Various designs of carved wooden statues in Yangôn.*

Religious Traditions

To be able to build a pagoda or monastery is the height of prestige for a Buddhist and is proof of his goodwill. Even the poorest Myanmar would seldom hesitate to donate something towards such a cause. Most volunteer their labour for construction, carrying bricks in the company of the people with whom they hope to be reunited in their next lives. A contribution to just the cost of renovation or maintenance is considered a great merit gained. Few ancient pagodas thus remain in their original forms.

It must seem to the visitor that the country is packed with pagodas, prayer halls and shrines of all sizes. Whitewashed stupas cling to the sides of cliffs, adorn the crest of high hilltops or nestle in shady groves. Even in the cities, one can see prayer halls or small pagodas wedged between high-rise apartment blocks in almost every neighbourhood.

A *hpongyi kyaung*, or "monastery", must be built in alignment with the east-west axis, a tradition established in the early eighteenth century. The pavilions have to be on a raised platform with an open patio around it called the *zingyan*, where the monks can walk up and down while meditating. Of the four stairs that lead up to the monastery, the two at the front would traditionally have been reserved for men and the two at the back for women but that is no longer the case today.

The doors and windows should open out to the south and north. The most important room, the shrine room, which is topped with the *pyatthat* tiered spire, should be set at the eastern end. *Pyatthat* roofs have existed since the time of the earliest Myanmar civilisations, as an incised stone from the Pyu period shows a building with tiered roofs. Wall paintings[85] and stone records of palace constructions from the Bagan period marked the use of these spire-like roofs that to this day are forbidden for secular use. Not many secular buildings were seen with the tiered roofs. However, Yangôn City Hall, Myoma High School, the Central Railway Station and the Karaweik Hotel are a few instances where the *pyatthat* tiered roof of religious and royal significance is used for non-religious buildings.

In the old days, only abbots and kings could enter the shrine room of the monastery, which is raised off the patio with short stairs from the east, south and north leading into it. Inside would be an ornate throne

Above: *Karaweik Hotel on Kandawgyi Lake, Yangôn. Note the tiered roofs.*

Opposite: *Devotees hoping to gain merit gather to sweep the grounds at Shwedagon Pagoda, Yangôn.*

with a Buddha image on it surrounded by vases of flowers, smaller images of the Buddha or *Rahans*[86], caskets of relics and other symbols of devotion.

Next to the shrin, connected by a small room, the *sanu hsaung*, where guest monks are received, is the large reception room known as the *hsaung ma gyi*. This part is roofed with *lai baw,* superimposed roofs that are usually set along the axis of each other in diminishing sizes in both odd and even numbers, up to four stacks on a monastery.

The reception room is divided into two along the centre by a wall called the *marabin* that is carved with motifs on both sides, exactly as the audience hall in a palace would be divided. Set against the partition wall on one side is the shrine with the Buddha images, where the throne would be in a palace. There, in a chair placed in front of the shrine, the abbot would address his devotees. Behind this partition is the bedroom of the abbot.

At the westernmost end is the *bawga hsaung*, separated from the reception hall by a few feet of the patio floor. This room is usually partitioned into three. One area would be used to store pots, chinaware and such, the middle area would be a place for younger monks and novices to sleep and the last room would serve as a larder.

Inside the monastery compound, which is normally spacious, is the *thein*, or "ordination hall", usually the first building to be set up on land designated for a monastery. The hall is demarcated by a short stone pillar capped with a lotus bud shape in each of the four corners. Women are forbidden to step within this boundary. There might also be an open rest house for pilgrims to stay in when they come to fast during religious holidays. A pavilion on or off the main monastery platform is built if necessary as a dormitory for younger monks. Mango and jackfruit trees provide shade on the bare grounds that are swept clean every morning and evening by novices or the *kappiya*, the layman head servant who looks after monastery affairs. He is also in charge of the *hpongyi kyaung tha*, the young boys sent to live and study at the monastery. Another monastic helper is the *hpothudaw*. Dressed in full white, he is one step away from becoming a novice.

A donor of a monastery is known as a *kyaung d'gar,* or "donor of the *kyaung*", and would be so addressed in conservative Myanmar society. In towns such as Pyay, Sale, Pakkoku, and Monywa, which are among the main trading centres of upper Myanmar, there are many wealthy families and thus many monasteries and pagodas. Some of the wooden monasteries are the wonder of present-day craftsmen who valiantly strive to match the architecture, carvings, attention to detail and sheer creativity of their predecessors.

Many monasteries and pagodas are situated in the dry, hot zone of central Myanmar, and are built with good air circulation and adequate shade in mind. Their eaves extend to a length that offers enough shade to the interior of halls. The door flaps are usually of the *ke-lar* type,

that is, wooden panels propped up from below with a staff, the typical style for windows in even the most common of bamboo houses. This ensures added protection from the sun since the flaps open upwards. Passages between the pavilions create breezeways.

Monasteries in Myanmar were not built solely for religious purposes. The survival of written Burmese and the high literacy rate in Myanmar can be attributed to the primary schools run by the monks. Each village has its own monastery and abbot and another one or two younger monks. The villagers take care of the needs of the monks who

Opposite: *Detail of the lace-like carvings adorning the roofs of a Buddhist monastery in Mawlamyine.*

Below: *A Buddhist monastery located in Bhamo.*

Right: *A young Buddhist monk looks out from the upper level of a monastery in Yangôn.*

in return officiate at ceremonies and teach young children to read and write. Monasteries also offer a sanctuary for orphaned, abandoned or homeless boys while nunneries do the same for girls. To keep better order, the children often remain as little nuns or novices. As it is not a lifetime commitment, they can choose to leave the religious order if they so wish, when they are older and able to fend for themselves. Even then, the monastery or nunnery is always considered "home".

Being centres of both social and religious affairs, monasteries need space for the public as well as privacy for monks. Thus, the plan of the monastery has to take into account the needs of the people and the school children as well as those of the monks. As a religious building, it must have distinct structures for *Sangha*[87] hierarchy.

The best examples of temples built in the traditional plan are the Shwe In Bin Monastery of Mandalay, and the Bargaya and Maha Aung Mye Bon Zan Monasteries of Inwa. Shwe In Bin Monastery was only built in 1890 but it adhered strictly to traditional rules of architecture, right down to the solid door flaps.

The Naw Man Monastery was originally a school building built in 1889 in Pazundaung Township, Yangôn. It was turned into a monastery through the addition of carvings and other traditional features. This extensive two-storey wooden building still stands although it is in a dilapidated state. The ground floor, with a balustrade of filigree ironwork, is open to the elements. It is still used for public ceremonies when the rough concrete floor would be covered with smooth rush mats and carpets. The monks' quarters are on the upper floor.

The most prestigious merit a Buddhist could aspire to achieve is to become a *paya d'gar,* "donor of a pagoda", by building a pagoda. There are two main types of pagoda. The conical stupa, usually a whitewashed or gilded structure that rises to a tapering point, has differently-shaped tiers topped with a gold, jewel-studded "umbrella". The other type of pagoda, the temple, is based on the cave structure. Some pagodas such as the Naga Hlaing Gu, "The Lair of the Dragon", in the northern

Below, left: Shwe In Bin Monastery in Mandalay was built according to strict architectural rules laid down by tradition.

Below, right: A monk stands at an entrance to Shwe In Bin Monastery.

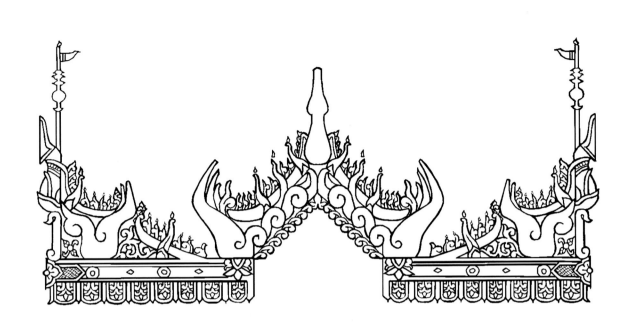

Above: *Detail of one level in the many tiers of the* pyatthat *roof.*

Below: *Shwe In Bin Monastery, Mandalay.*

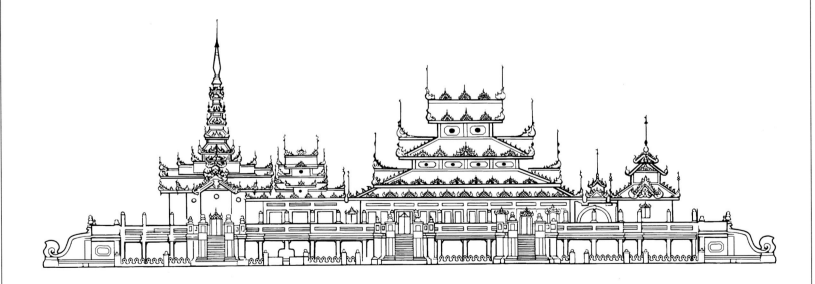

outskirts of Yangôn combine the two, a cave underneath a stupa. This pagoda is believed to have existed since the eleventh century. Similar pagodas are the Kaba Aye Pagoda where the Sixth Buddhist Synod was held, the Tooth Relic Pagoda and the Mahawizaya Pagoda, all of which are located in Yangôn.

A pagoda that departs from the usual architectural norms is the Thanbodday in the prosperous town of Monywa, 84 miles northeast of Mandalay on the Chindwin River. The Thanbodday has been likened to the Borobudur of Indonesia. It is complex and minutely detailed, with a central stupa surrounded by small shrines set on several levels of encircling terraces. Each shrine houses a small Buddha image set in a niche. The base platform is dotted with pillars both high and low, set upon shrines and lined with yet more minute images. The Thanbodday is believed to contain more than 580,000 Buddha images of varying sizes from an inch high to seven feet tall.

Across a stone pathway from the spire is the ordination hall, a huge brick pavilion with outer walls that are covered from top to bottom with scenes of the *Jataka* tales. The figures in high relief are painted in a rainbow of pastel colours. The artists have included such charming touches as ladies peering over a screen, children at play and the hindquarters of a dog sneaking through a door. A more whimsical touch is the Chinese pavilion donated by Aw Boon Haw, one of the Haw Par brothers who had made their fortune in Burma with their famous Tiger Balm cream. Their two figures in western suits stand guard at

this hall, expressions of quiet satisfaction evident in their faces. The icons of their product, two tigers in painted plaster, are frozen in the act of clawing over the top of a high wall. The whole pagoda complex is guarded not as is usual by masonry lions, but by two gigantic figures of the most noble of creatures: the white elephant.

The most splendid of all pagodas is surely the Shwedagon of Yangôn. Eight strands of the Buddha's hair are believed to have been enshrined within the structure during his lifetime. In earlier centuries, the pagoda was but a plain stupa reportedly only 60 feet high. Bigger spires were built over time to enclose the smaller ones like shells. The first time it was gilded over completely was in 1460, when its height had already been raised to nearly 300 feet. Queen Shin Saw Pu,

Opposite, left: *The Tooth Relic Pagoda in Yangôn is an example of a pagoda that incorporates both the cave and stupa structure.*

Opposite, right: *Thanbodday Pagoda in Monywa has been compared to Indonesia's Borobudur .*

Below: *Detail of a tiger at Thanbodday Pagoda.*

Right: *Statue of Aw Boon Haw at Thanbodday Pagoda. He is one of the Haw Par brothers, made rich and famous by the success of their Tiger Balm cream.*

Left: *The magnificent Shwedagon Pagoda in Yangôn is a grand, awe-inspiring structure.*

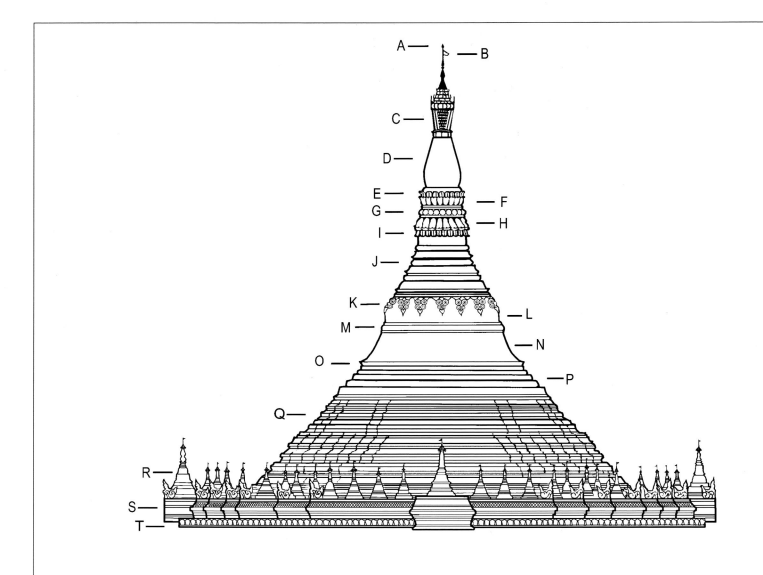

A	Diamond Orb	K	Flower Sprigs
B	Gold Banner	L	Inverted Alms Bowl
C	Umbrella	M	Bosom Wrap
D	Banana Bud	N	Bell
E	Tender Lotus	O	Rim of the Bell
F	Upturned Lotus	P	Brass Coils
G	Glass Baubles	Q	Octagonal Ridges
H	Inverted Lotus	R	Small Stupas
I	Tender Lotus	S	Flower Platform
J	Embossed Wrap	T	Royal Footwear

Opposite: *An illustration showing the various parts of a pagoda.*

Above: *The statue of the Manoke Thiha guards Shwedagon Pagoda in Yangôn.*

known to the Mon as Queen Banya Thau, a well-loved monarch who had reigned for seven years in lower Myanmar, donated her weight in gold, 91 pounds, for this purpose. It was beaten into sheets and then lacquered onto the surface.

The Shwedagon now stands 326 feet high with the *Hti Taw,* "Royal Umbrella", measuring in at 16 feet 3 inches. The amount of gold on the spire alone is calculated to exceed three tonnes. Several earthquakes damaged the umbrella, which was repaired and encrusted with more jewels each time. A number of kings have donated gold, jewels and even complete umbrellas amounting to about a tonne of metal, most of it gold. The discarded umbrellas are encased in plaster and set up on the Shwedagon platform as *hti* pagodas.

 The circumference for the tip of the *hti,* called the "Diamond Orb", was measured at 31 inches when the *hti* was repaired in the 1970s. A count conducted at the same time found the *hti* decorated with 4,351 diamonds totalling 1,800 carats. The diamond set at its peak was a 76-carat solitaire.

The diamond orb is supported by a gold staff and a gold banner more than two feet wide and four feet long. These are encrusted with 1,098 diamonds and 1,338 precious stones such as rubies, emeralds and sapphires, most of them still set in the original jewellery that the people had donated. The pieces of jewellery on the banner alone numbered 5,390.

When a new *hti* was set in place in April of 1999[88], a great many more jewels had been added. An additional 79,659 pieces of jewellery were attached to the *hti* in 1999, bringing the total to a staggering 83,850 pieces. Most people, in a more personal gesture of devotion, donated what they were wearing when they came to the pagoda. Rings, bracelets and a total of 4,016 gold bells were welded onto the *hti* or threaded through thick wires of gold and firmly tied around the support pole, which was also replaced with one encrusted with diamonds. The new frame was also reinforced with steel.

Each step in the installation of a new *hti* has to be done according to rigid rules, one of which is that no noise must be made while inserting the central pole into the socket, a task that must be accomplished in one movement. Adjusting the pole by lifting it and putting it in place again is forbidden according to old manuscripts.

A stupa by tradition is built upwards in several sections, the height and width of which are determined by its overall design. The basic stages in building a stupa, according to the plan of the Shwedagon, are described in the following paragraphs.

The base is called the *Hpa-nut Taw*, "Royal Footwear". Next comes the 21-foot high *Pan Tin Khone*, a square "Flower-placing Platform" on which there are 64 gilded stupas. There is a corridor between these smaller stupas and the main spire where only men are allowed to traverse. In a shrine on this corridor circling the base of the shrine is a Buddha image named Padamya Myet Shin, the "Living Eye of the Ruby". As only men can walk on this upper terrace, a camera and television screen on the lower platform give the female pilgrims a chance to worship the image. On a corner of the *Pan Tin Khone*, to one side of the western pavilion, there is a figure of King Okkalappa looking out over the platform. According to legend, it was he who built the pagoda. Standing on either side are the figures of his parents, the King of the Celestials and the Lady Mai Lamu, a maiden born from the *lamu* fruit. Both are offered fresh flowers and light every day and night. From this upper terrace rise the ascending octagonal ridges of the *Pyitsaya*, which effectively connects the square base with the circular form of the spire as it rises higher. The octagonal shape also symbolises the Eight-Fold Path to Nirvana.

Over the *Pyitsaya* are brass coils, widely-spaced ridges that end with the graceful tilt of the *Khaung Laung Nar*, "Rim of the Bell". Over this rises in a smooth, graceful curve the *Khaung Laung*, "The Bell" itself. The upper part of this Bell is somewhat rounded and resembles an inverted bowl. Indeed, it is named the *Thabaik Hmauk*, "Inverted Alms Bowl". Between the Bell and the Inverted Bowl are two lines called the *Yin Hsee*, the "Bosom Wrap". Tapering sprigs of stylised flowers in gold hang along the upper circumference of the bowl. Such flowers are called *Pan Hswai* or "Hanging Flowers".

Right: *Various smaller stupas ring the large main stupa at the Shwedagon Pagoda in Yangôn.*

Upwards from the edge of the *Thabaik Hmauk* are ridges called *Hpaung Yit*, which taper in size until they reach a line of inverted petal motifs called the *Kyar Nu*, "Tender Lotus Petals". Above are larger inverted lotus petals, the *Kyar Hmaut*. A band set with half-spheres has the name *Ywai Lone*, "Glass Baubles". Above this come the bigger petals in an upright position, *Kyar Hlan*, the "Upright Lotus". This is followed again by a ring of the small Tender Lotus Petals, then the *Nget Pyaw Hpu* or "Banana Bud" that finally ends at the base of the metal *Hti Taw* or "Royal Umbrella".

The staff that holds the diamond orb, *Sein Hpu,* and the gold banner, *Nget Myat Nar,* is known as "Where the Noble Bird Rests". It is based on the *Hsat Tha Hpu*, named after a flower that has an elegant elongated bud. This gem-studded bud alone is eight feet tall.

Every ten years, the whole spire is encased in bamboo scaffolding that gracefully conforms to the shape of the stupa, and more gold leaf is applied. Some parts are covered with gold leaf. In other places, gold plates are attached with screws. Runoff rainwater from the platform is collected in tanks and auctioned to a few prominent goldsmiths who would try to extract the gold.

It is not only the towering shimmering spire that promotes awe; the four main pavilions on each point of the compass and the other *zayat* rest houses on the edge of the walk surrounding the Shwedagon all have unique architectural styles. The best of Myanmar wood carving can be seen on the "bats' wings" connecting the pillars. Good examples may be seen at the Rakhine Tazaung, a pavilion donated, so it reads over the entrance, by The Western Country's Rakhine Merchants Association. The one next to it is of a similar structure but vastly different form, especially in the *pyatthat* tiered-roofs. They stand between the west and south entrances. Behind these pavilions are many others, smaller ones tucked into corners and bigger ones looking out over the cityscape.

Not all spires of pagodas in Myanmar are covered in gold, although most are. Many are whitewashed and some are covered with glass mosaic. There is one, a little beyond the southern stairs of the Shwedagon, which is entirely covered with shards of glass; the pavilions, the walls and the stupa itself. It is aptly called the Diamond Flame Pagoda. The shape of the stupa also does not conform to the traditions described.

Above: *The diamond orb and gold banner of a* hti, *also known as "Where the Noble Bird Rests".*

Left: *The glass-covered spire of the Diamond Flame Pagoda.*

Below: *Detail of a glass figure at the Diamond Flame Pagoda.*

Right: *Kaung Hmu Daw Pagoda, built in Sagaing in 1636, is a departure from the usual architecture of pagodas in Myanmar.*

Another stupa that varies a great degree from any accepted norm is the Kaung Hmu Daw Pagoda of Sagaing, a whitewashed dome built in 1636 in the style of the Maha Zedi of Sri Lanka.

Another is Ah-lain Nga Hsint Pagoda in the Insein Township of Yangôn. It was built according to the recurring dreams of a monk, U Thuriya[89], who was born in 1915. He was said to have built more than a thousand pagodas all over the country. This particular pagoda, which looks like a Russian cathedral, was built exactly as the one he so often saw in his dream. In 1958, the land was cleared, the foundation laid and the pagoda built to his specifications. Needless to say, the onion-shaped dome is topped with the traditional umbrella.

It has astonished strangers, and will likely continue to do so, that the Myanmar people have less regard for beautifying their own homes than their pagodas. But such is the way of life, to take pride in what one can do to gain merit for future lives. In doing this, Myanmar throughout the centuries have taken the arts of their neighbours to incorporate into their own designs.

Since centuries past, trade and war have created bonds between the kingdoms of Burma and neighbouring countries. Arts mingled, cultures merged. When the British began to encroach on Asian lands and conquered India, they brought their own culture with their armies. It did not take long before they made their way to Burma. Although the British departed in 1948 when Burma gained her independence, traces of the colonial era remain not in Myanmar culture but in buildings, historical reminders of brick and mortar.

Left: *The unconventional-looking Ah-lain Nga Hsint Pagoda in Yangôn was built by the monk U Thuriya to resemble a pagoda that he kept seeing in his dreams.*

THE TWAIN MEET

During the colonial era, British culture could not gain a foothold in Burma as the people held on rigidly to their own traditions and beliefs. However, in some cases, western architectural styles did meld with Burmese designs to produce charming results.

Examples of western architecture remain in the areas earliest colonised, especially in towns where the colonial administration was centred such as Mawlamyine (Moulmein), the first capital of the British, set up after the First Anglo-Burmese War of 1824. Yangôn too was lost to the British after the war. It was handed back to the Burma in 1826 only after partial payment of an exorbitant compensation of ten million rupees, or one million pounds sterling, to the East India Company. The balance was paid in 1932.

Yangôn, or "Rangoon" as it was mispronounced by the British, was once called Dagon by the Burmese and Lagun by the Mon. It was a small fishing town known only because it happened to be the site where the famous pagoda, Shwedagon, was located. Legends about how this great pagoda came into being tell of the Buddha giving eight of his hairs to two Mon brothers. On their arrival in Lagun, the brothers presented the hairs to the king who ruled the nearby kingdom of Okkalappa. The king enshrined the precious gifts in a small, 60-foot-high stupa on a hill called Thainguttara.

The first westerners to mention the pagoda and the town were the Venetian gem trader, Gasparo Balbi, and the Englishman, Ralph Fitch, who both visited Dagon in the sixteenth century. Balbi arrived in November of 1583 during the light festival of Tazaungdaing, and thought the heavily-populated town to be as festive at all times. He was greatly impressed with the pagoda, where long stairs lead up to the platform on which he saw richly-gilded pavilions, a huge bronze bell and a golden spire rising to the sky.

By 1752, the Mon of lower Myanmar, with French assistance, had retaken not only lower Myanmar but also conquered the Burmese domain of Inwa. The conquering king, Banya Dala, left a governor at Inwa and returned to Bago. However, within months, a Burmese rebellion led by Alaungpaya was launched in upper Myanmar.

After three years of war with the Mon, King Alaungpaya, the founder of the third Burmese empire, finally emerged victorious. He took Dagon in 1755 and in the process completely destroyed the seaport of Thanlyin (Syriam) because he did not wish to see a Mon stronghold of any importance remain. One of the ruins seen today in Thanlyin is a church that had been built in 1750, only to be destroyed by Alaungpaya five years after its completion.

The Burmese king wanted another port to take the place of Thanlyin and decided that there was no town more suitable for that purpose than the one graced by the presence of a great pagoda. He hoped that there would no longer be any enmity, at least from the Mon, and he changed the name of Dagun to Yangôn, "End of Strife"[90]. With Thanlyin razed to the ground, Yangôn indeed became the biggest port in the country.

Alaungpaya laid out a town plan on the bank of the Yangôn River, covering perhaps not more than an eighth of a square mile. Its centre lay to the east of the Sule Pagoda, considered the centre of the present-day city. At the time, the Sule Pagoda was on swampy ground, standing on a laterite mound surrounded by two creeks that flowed into the Yangôn River. At times, the area would be under deep water.

Beyond the town walls, where there is dry land today, there were once ponds and creeks and the isolated villages of Kyimyin Daing (Kemmendine) and Pazundaung, one in the east, the other west. Within the stockade, houses had to be built high on stilts since the river overflowed in the monsoon season. Some Europeans had already settled in Yangôn but they were used to more solid foundations and viewed the high houses with some apprehension. The roads were dirt lanes with drains dug on either side. Drinking water was obtained from wells dug outside the stockade. Within the stockade, floods were common and any wells dug there would be contaminated by water from the river. In the surrounding forests, there were dangerous wild creatures, elephants, crocodiles and tigers.

By the end of the eighteenth century, French and Portuguese influences in the Burmese court of Inwa were causing tensions between the Burmese and the British. Yangôn was by that time a flourishing seaport and Michael Symes, the Envoy of Britain posted to the Court of Ava in 1795, thought it the best in the eastern world. Unfortunately, the intrigues of court, power plays, the ineptitude of some monarchs due to the tradition of royal in-breeding[91] and foreign incursions were all too soon to play a part in the serious diminishing of the power of the Burmese empire, which Symes once believed to have been second only to that of China.

The urgency with which foreign traders established commercial footholds in Burma added to the turmoil of the royal court. The result was the First Anglo-Burmese War of 1824. It started with a border incident in the Rakhine involving some workers of the East India Company and ended with the British being ceded the provinces of Assam, Manipur, Rakhine and the Taninthayi Coast.

By 1827, the British had begun to extract teak on a large scale from Taninthayi, with the first sawmills in the country being set up in Mawlamyine. It is a place conveniently situated at the mouth of the Thanlwin River that was and still is used for little else apart from logging. Thick teak jungles line both sides of the river. Timber merchants flocked there and mills grew like mushrooms to take advantage of the apparently inexhaustible supply of teak from the region, one of the main resources in Burma that attracted the British.

Pages 116-117: *The spire of Sule Pagoda rises in the background as monks go about their daily activities.*

Opposite: *Mahawizaya Pagoda, located not far from the Shwedagon in Yangôn, is a more recent addition to the city's many pagodas.*

Left: *Sule Pagoda, in Yangôn, is said to have been built more than 2,000 years ago but has undergone multiple renovations since that time.*

Located further south, Myeik (Mergui) was a place important to the security of the country. Not easily accessible from the central government of whoever was in power, it was once a hotbed of intrigue and shady deals hatched by even shadier characters such as the British pirate Samuel (Siamese) White. In his day, during the seventeenth century, the town was cosmopolitan, more so than any other city in Burma. Although it was under the rule of the Siamese king at the time, Indians, Chinese, Thais, Malays, Europeans and Burmese mixed and traded freely in the town.

Two of the landmarks in Myeik are the Theindaw Gyi Pagoda, standing on the highest hill overlooking the town, and a teak mansion, once the Deputy Commissioner's residence, located a little lower down the hillside. The mansion had been occupied at one time by Maurice Collis, the colonial administrator who wrote several books on Burma. Known for years as the Big Black House, its history is appropriately sprinkled with tales of hauntings by ghosts of people massacred during Samuel White's time. Between the pagoda and the Big Black House is a brick treasury and, next to it, a huge office complex with delicate scroll-edged roofs and wooden-louvred windows. From this hill, one can look down on the port, walled behind the saddle-shaped Pitaw Patik Island. Beyond this rises the misty heights of King's Island, with peaks rising over 3,000 feet high. To the north, the open sea stretches out toward an empty horizon.

During the two years of British occupation, hundreds of pagodas and shrines around the Shwedagon were broken into in and looted. Fortunately, the Shwedagon had been encased at least seven times by then. Despite multiple attempts, it proved impossible to penetrate. A 25-tonne bell donated to the pagoda in 1779 by King Singu (r. 1776–1782) in memory of his father King Hsinbyushin (r. 1763–1776) was about to be shipped away by the British in 1824 but it slipped into the river. Six fruitless months of effort to haul it out followed before Burmese residents of the town asked permission to try to recover the bell, the condition being that if they were successful, the bell would

Right: *The Big Black House in Myeik, once the residence of colonial-era administrator and writer Maurice Collis.*

be returned to the Shwedagon. They lashed the bell to bamboo rafts at low tide and it rose as the tide came in. It was triumphantly carried back to the pagoda, where it still hangs.

Before British rule, a *Myowun*, "town minister", resided in Yangôn to represent the Burmese king, who lived in upper Myanmar. In 1830, a Resident Agent, Colonel Henry Burney, was installed there to look after British interests.

In 1841 King Tharyarwaddy, who had overthrown his brother King Bodawpaya and his common-born queen Mai Nu in 1837, arrived in Yangôn from Inwa on his golden royal barge with a retinue of fifteen thousand, a further nine thousand preceding him. He made offerings at the Shwedagon and re-gilded the spire while holding great festivals. It was a political move rather than a pilgrimage. His pomp and ceremony was meant to lift the morale of the people of lower Burma, as some parts were under British rule and the Burmese capital was too far to the north.

Left: *The south entrance to Shwedagon Pagoda, Yangôn, guarded by* chinthe.

Below: *A shiny bronze image of the Buddha at Shwedagon Pagoda.*

Tharyarwaddy moved Yangôn further inland, about a mile and a quarter from the river, to protect it from floods. With the Shwedagon Pagoda at its northeast corner, the almost-square town was fortified with walls surrounded by a moat. Thirty wells were dug. The king departed early the next year to return to Amarapura. In February 1843, he sent a 40-tonne bronze bell to the pagoda where it still hangs in the north-eastern corner. He also built a new wharf for his use[92], with a road leading from it to the western entrance of the Shwedagon. The Lanmadaw or "Royal Main Road" still exists to this day although his town lasted only ten years.

Colesworthey Grant, a British artist who came to Yangôn in 1846 recorded that the most conspicuous building on the riverfront of Yangôn was the house of Mr. G.S. Mannook, an Armenian trader whose father had built it in 1828. "It consists of six compartments in a line, each with a gable end to it, and the whole is constructed of wood. The windows have Venetian shades... but not an atom of glass. No glass, it appears, is permitted to any other dwelling in Burmah than the king's palace!". The artist made a great number of pencil sketches, once getting arrested by the Burmese authorities on suspicion of spying while he was drawing the Signal Pagoda near the southern entrance of the Shwedagon. He was let free after a morning's captivity, having been asked to make a drawing of a marionette. However, his sketches were mostly of pagodas, "so numerous, and though similar in general form, yet so varied in character and detail". He wrote about his visit to the "Shooay-tagon" one evening, but he and his European companion were not allowed onto the platform. They would have needed special permission from the head "Ponngee", or *Hpongyi*, a Buddhist monk.

Another notable building, the residence of Captain Hugh Brown, "merchant, post master,... European shipwright, engaged in building a ship for the king, was constructed almost entirely of brick, stone and iron... from the foundation upwards it is of massive brick work". Due to its thick walls, heavy iron doors and "small embrasure-like windows with their iron bars and solid iron shutters", it became known as "The Prison". Strangely enough, it had a thatch roof. It stood on the first street that ran parallel with the river, probably Strand Road. It had been

Left: A beautifully decorated barge on Kandawgyi Lake, Yangôn.

built long before the First Anglo-Burmese War of 1824 and at that time was used as the headquarters of General Sir Archibald Campbell.

Repairs to the house needed special permission from the king, which Grant wrote was difficult to obtain. He noted the "motley appearance of Rangoon streets" and that "it does not require looking far here to be assured you are in a timber country". The British Residency looked "more like a large barn", with gable ends and a thatch roof. He admired the houses of the Burmese as well as the *zayat* rest houses and the monasteries, but was severely disappointed how indifferently the gardens were kept, without flowering bushes although planted with fruit trees.

At best mistrustful of each other, relations between the British and the Burmese deteriorated swiftly. The British were eager to extend their empire. Their envoys were arrogant and the mercantile traders in Yangôn a wily lot, good at finding loopholes in the regulations. King Bagan (r. 1846–1853) succeeded Tharyarwaddy and started out as an able ruler but he soon became more interested in drink and animal sports than with state affairs. Officials on both sides were insolent to their counterparts. In 1852, the Second Anglo-Burmese War began,

Below and right: *Various styles of wooden-shuttered windows in Yangôn.*

Opposite: *An Old Burmese house in Yangôn lies in the cool shade of coconut trees.*

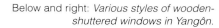

resulting in the annexation by the British of the fertile Bago provinces, including Yangôn. With popular support, King Bagan's younger brother Mindon swiftly deposed of him and ascended the throne in 1853.

By the end of the Second Anglo-Burmese War, the British were confident enough of their foothold in the country that they began to construct buildings that were sturdier than the previous barn- or prison-like residences. However, it was not until the 1870s that large-scale construction work started.

Lord Dalhousie, the Governor General, drew up an administrative plan, according to which the province of Yangôn was to be governed by a Commissioner. Captain Arthur Phayre was the first man appointed to the position with Captain T.P. Sparks assigned as his deputy. The first problem they faced was to plan the town on a new, more convenient layout and to make it large enough so that it could develop into a proper city. King Tharyarwaddy's town on high ground was turned into the cantonment, or army quarters. To make way for the barracks, many pagodas within the fortified walls of the city were destroyed. One of the pagodas, donated by Queen Shun Saw Pu, had been enshrined with solid gold artefacts. These and treasures from other pagodas were looted and taken back to Britain. Part of the loot can still be seen in the Victoria and Albert Museum of London.

Dr. William Montgomerie, a Superintendent Surgeon with the troops, had been posted to Singapore while it was being planned by Sir Stamford Raffles. There, he had served as Secretary to the Town Committee, so he possessed "considerable experience" in city planning. The plan he proposed was modified by Lieutenant A. Fraser of the Bengal Engineers to cover a larger area but even that was insufficient to accommodate the proper development of the city. Fraser's second plan extended it beyond the Sule Pagoda, effectively turning the pagoda into the city centre.

Both Montgomerie and Fraser laid out the city in a grid pattern, with main roads running parallel to the river and minor roads running across. Unfortunately, the lots cramped between the minor roads were narrow, in contrast to the wide streets and large square lots of Mandalay, which was built in 1859. By comparison, Yangôn seemed to be huddled close to the river. The rigid grid plan meant narrow, long apartments that had windows only at the front and back.

Timber pilings were erected along the river on a large scale to build a bund. The swamp around Sule Pagoda was drained and filled in with rubbish from the town and earth from the outer suburbs. The areas outside the town centre were neither filled nor drained for many years, leaving residents to live in highly unsanitary conditions. Proper sanitation was also not available, especially in the crowded quarters of Indian labourers. It is therefore not suprising that until the 1920s, Yangôn suffered several epidemics of dysentery, plague, typhoid, smallpox and cholera.

Water was also a problem as that drawn from Kandawgyi Lake, or "Royal Lake", turned out to be unpotable. Another source had to be found and the search led to Victoria Lake, later called Inya Lake. However, the supply of water that the lake could provide proved to be insufficient. A new source was later found at the Hlawga Reservoir, 17 miles away. It is still in use today.

Brick buildings went up, in almost the same architectural style as was fashionable in England at the time. Kerosene lampposts were erected along the main streets and Indian workers would go from post to post each evening to light the street lamps. Cheap Indian labour was brought in so much so that Yangôn had the look of an Indian city. By the mid nineteenth century, the Indian work force had helped build many offices and residences in the city, sometimes beautiful and sometimes ugly but all of them startling to Burmese eyes.

The Burmese had rarely seen doubled-storeyed buildings, let alone three-storeyed secular buildings thickly walled with brick. The turrets, Corinthian and Doric pillars, arches, domes and red brick with gold trim burst upon Burmese eyes that had previously only been exposed to dainty *Kanote* flowers and ornate tiered roofs.

The locals were both repelled and charmed. As their priority was in religious monuments, the Burmese began to use the nicer western design elements in monasteries, which they began to build in brick instead of timber. This was done not only because it was the "latest fashion", but also because it took longer to carve in wood than to mould stucco. There was also the danger posed by fire. Thus it came to be that a short time later, the Burmese king himself led his nobles and the wealthy in donating brick pavilions and monasteries that combined eastern designs with those of the west.

Above: *Strand Road, Yangôn.*

The influx of Indian labour also meant that wealthy members of their community funded the building of mosques and Hindu temples. When the British administrators planned the city, they had given plots of land, exempted from taxation, to various religious communities for the building of places of worship.

Churches, a common sight in Yangôn as well as remote border towns, were built by Christian missionaries who had preceded the armies of Queen Victoria. Missionary work had started in southern Burma around the time of the Second Anglo-Burmese War under the leadership of Bishop Paul Ambrose Bigandet. By the time of his death in 1894, 32 missions had been established. Although western culture did not penetrate Burmese Buddhist society, missionary teachings changed the lives of other ethnic peoples living in remote regions. They became educated, but at the loss of their cultural heritage.

Reverend Andoniram Judson and his wife, among the first American missionaries to be sent out by the American Baptist Mission, arrived in Burma in 1813. The church Judson set up in Mawlamyine is a revered as well as an important historical sight. Judson, who had at one time been imprisoned in Ava for two years, is considered one of the foremost educators of early modern Myanmar. His works include a Burmese-English dictionary as well as a translation of the Bible.

Other immigrants who arrived in Burma around this time, apart from the Indians, included those from two provinces in China. The hardy labourers from Canton wore short-sleeved jackets while the traders from Fukien wore the more elegant long sleeves, a fashion indicating that they did no manual labour. The Burmese distinguished between them by calling the Cantonese "Short Sleeves" and the Fukienese "Long Sleeves".

The Fukienese temple built in 1861 on the corner of Sint Oh Dan, or the "Street of the Glazed Pots", and Strand Road in Yangôn is a beautiful example of Chinese architecture. Artist Talbot Kelly, who visited Yangôn in 1904, was particularly impressed by the temple, describing it with apparent delight: "the roof... highly glazed tiles of many colours... finials composed of richly ornate dragons in porcelain... the interior is rich... timbers lacquered or carved like ivory... beams and joints being completely perforated almost like filigree work, then picked out in gold and vermilion".

A Cantonese temple stands on the corner of Mahabandoola and what used to be Latter Street, now renamed Latha or "Shining Moon". Smaller, and less ornate, it was built in 1829. This temple is almost spartan with slim, unadorned square pillars, slender beams, a soft grey exterior and gently-sloping roofs. Inside, an old, gnarled tree climbs out of a hole in the roof especially cut for it. Across the street are numerous goldsmith shops, their long glass counters filled with shimmering jewellery, owned by the descendents of the immigrants from Pyay Gyi, "The Big Country", as China is called.

A small community of Jews built a small but richly-decorated synagogue on 26th Street of Yangôn. It remains in use to this day, not by the Myanmar Jewish community as it no longer exists but by expatriates living in the city. In many towns in Myanmar, pagodas, churches, temples and mosques stand amicably in the same neighbourhood, often within sight of each other. The different religious communities usually stick to their own kind and there are few clashes between them.

Opposite, top: *Detail of the architectural features on a western-styled building on Pansodan Road, Yangôn.*

Opposite, bottom: *St. Anthony's Roman Catholic Church in Yangôn.*

Left: *St. Mary's Roman Catholic Cathedral in Yangôn.*

Below: *A headstone in an English cemetery, Yangôn.*

In the early twentieth century, Yangôn began to lose the little ambience it had of being a Burmese town. There were many Indian and Chinese residents in the downtown area. Talbot Kelly said that his first impression upon seeing the city was of "the Indian character of the place". He seemed impressed with the dress and demeanour of the Burmese, whom he described as walking modestly and attractive in appearance. He noted that they were always well-dressed and that their purple-black hair was luxurious; the women placed flowers in the coils of their hair "in a very coquettish" manner.

However, Kelly bemoaned the fact that although the *shikoh*[93] was a part of the Burmese culture, the Burmese he met declined to *shikoh* to Europeans and passed by "with an air of unconscious indifference" while other races politely and respectfully *salaam*-ed them. He noticed that he saw the Burmese only near or at the Shwedagon and other pagodas and monasteries. They lived in their own neighbourhoods of traditional wooden houses, away from the dockside. In the town centre, new western-styled buildings changed the face of Yangôn forever.

The red-bricked, yellow-stuccoed buildings of the Secretariat, the High Courts and the Yangôn General Hospital today look picturesque with their ornate architecture and majestic with their lofty bearing and massive size. However, when these buildings had just been completed, they were greeted with ridicule by the general public as being ugly and too ornate. The Law Courts even suffered being the brunt of a joke that it had been designed by a convict with a grudge against the judge.

The Secretariat is built around a courtyard and occupies one entire block. A huge dome over the front entrance is the dominating feature.

Construction was begun in 1890 and completed in 1905. It too was greeted with derision for its ornate design, although with nostalgia and grace that time alone can nurture, it is now accepted as a magnificent example of colonial architecture. Cloaked in the red-bricked dignity befitting its role, it still serves as the nerve centre of the government,

Opposite: Reverend Andoniram Judson's Church in Mawlamyine is of great significance as the first Baptist church in Myanmar.

Below: The Fukienese Temple, a building much admired by artist Talbot Kelly during his visit to Yangôn in the early 1900s.

as it has since its birth. It was also the site of an unsurpassed tragedy in the history of modern Myanmar. In July 1947, General Aung San[94], the young and forceful leader who was the hero of the independence movement, was assassinated along with five members of his cabinet,. They were gunned down while in a meeting. Independence was granted six months later.

A new general hospital replaced the original wooden buildings in 1911. It was the first building in the country to use reinforced concrete. By modern health standards, it is now far outmoded. Nevertheless, doctors and nurses have a strong affection for its sprawling corridors and warrens of rooms, even as they grumble about the inconveniences. Set behind the central dome is the original roomy elevator, still creaking up and down majestically in its cage of delicate iron grilles. Wide marble stairways run around it up to the top floor. A pretty spiral staircase, called a "Cat's Winding Ladder" in Burmese, continues upwards to the glass roof, which gives ample light to the interior.

Below: *Detail of the images of Hindu deities to be found at a temple in Yangôn.*

Right: *A colourful Hindu temple, Yangôn.*

Opposite: *The spires of a mosque in Mawlamyine.*

Other buildings dear to the hearts of professionals are the Convocation Hall and the University Central Library, completed in 1927. All these campus landmarks have achieved immortality, having been woven into the plots of countless novels that often feature a beautiful tree of great age, the *thit-poke* tree (*Dalbergia kurzii*),which stands not far from the Convocation Hall.

The headquarters of the Irrawaddy Flotilla Company, built in 1933, has Corinthian columns two floors tall. The street on which it stands, once named Phayre Street, is now called Pansodan Street, "The Street of Fabric Dyers". The Irrawaddy Flotilla and Burmese Steam Navigation Company, Limited, sometimes abbreviated as the I.F., started operations in 1862 and at the height of its success, ran over 500 vessels on the Ayeyarwady and Chindwin Rivers and along the Taninthayi Coast. The building now houses the Inland Water Transport Board.

Next to it was once Grindlay's Bank. A four-storeyed, massive building with simple lines, its unadorned half-pillars are spanned with

walls of lacy masonry. It was later used as the National Museum until a new museum was completed on Pyay Road in 1996.

On the corner of Pansodan Street and Strand Road is the Port Authority Building, with its single high tower and a row of small decorative stucco anchors along the front. Not too far away is Bank No. 2, an austere, spartan building seemingly out-of-place among the graceful pillars of its neighbours. Much further north are the two Internal Revenue office buildings facing each other across Pansodan.

The Customs House, built in 1915, is the successor to the first building that went up on the same site when Yangôn emerged as a port.

The imposing City Hall stands next to the Sule Pagoda and across from Mahabandoola Garden. A Burmese political leader, U Ba Pe, affectionately known to all as Elder Uncle Ba Pe, had proposed to the Municipal Committee that there was a need for a city hall. At that time, the Municipality office had been situated in the Rowe and Company building. The Municipal Committee bought the adjoining plot of land from the British Government for 169,182 rupees and in 1913 held a competition for the best design for a new city hall. The first prize of £300 was won by Mr. L.A. McClumpha.

Construction was postponed due to World War I and it was only in 1926 that work on the building began under the supervision of Mr. Bray, an architect. Public demands that traditional features of Burmese architecture be incorporated led to U Tin, a Burmese architect trained in the west, adding to the original design and overseeing construction. He travelled to Bagan and other typically Burmese towns to note the details of pagodas and wooden monasteries, which he later incorporated into the revised design. The new City Hall was formally opened by His Excellency Sir Archibald Cochrane, Governor of Burma, on 15 June 1936. Its cost was 180,000 rupees.

Opposite: *The distinctive red-and-yellow façade of the High Court building in Yangôn.*

Left: *The Secretariat building in Yangôn was the target of much ridicule when it was first completed.*

Pages 138-139: *Construction of the City Hall building in Yangôn was postponed when World War I broke out. It was finally completed in 1936.*

Mahabandoola Garden, a rectangular park in front of the City Hall, was formerly called Fytche Square, after Albert Fytche, the British Chief Commissioner between 1867 and 1871. After independence, its name was changed to honour the Burmese hero, General Mahabandoola, who had fought valiantly against great odds in the First Anglo-Burmese War of 1824. In this park stands the Myanmar Independence Monument. Viewed from the top, it looks exactly the same as the design on the top left of the Myanmar national flag chosen at independence: one big five-pointed star surrounded by five smaller ones, symbolising the Union of Burma and the five main ethnicities, which after 1962 was more accurately raised to seven. Sule Pagoda and the High Courts are situated along two different sides of the garden. On another side, shady trees obscure traffic on the narrow Merchant Street.

Rowe and Company's departmental store was once located in the ornate, towering corner block next to the City Hall. Built in 1910, it shares the same style as the Secretariat. It was once the place to shop; even the Burmese ladies who resented British rule would not buy their china anywhere else. *Tike* means "brick building" and Yo Tike, as Rowe's was called by the Burmese, rapidly came to symbolise prestige among the affluent in every town that had an outlet of this hugely successful chain store[95].

Bogyoke Aung San Market, formerly named Scott's Market after Municipal Commissioner Gavin Scott, has been a popular shopping destination since it opened in 1926. Generations of lovers have arranged to rendezvous under the clock at Scott's. It is a huge complex with several wings extending from the side of the main high-ceiling

hall. Lined with hundreds of stalls in true bazaar fashion, salesgirls on platforms sell wares that are crammed behind low glass counters. With few shops open during the years of the disastrous Burmese Way to Socialism, from 1962 to 1988, it became a favourite pastime for the young to stroll around this market on a Saturday morning. Now, the market is a tourist attraction offering crafts and jewellery, a sprawling Oriental bazaar.

The decaying red-bricked railway headquarters not too far from Bogyoke Aung San Market is one of the best examples of western architecture in the city. Its row of windows, framed with filigree railings and hooded with matching awnings, breaks the monotony of the façade, giving it an exotic charm quite unlike that of any other building. It stands in view of the Sule Pagoda.

Opposite: *The former headquarters of the Irrawaddy Flotilla Company on Pansodan Street, Yangôn.*

Bottom left: *The Port Authority Building (right), located just down the road from the headquarters of the Irrawaddy Flotilla Company.*

Bottom right: *The red-bricked Customs House, Yangôn.*

Also on Sule Pagoda Road stands the ornate premises of the Government Pharmacy with its bay windows on the first floor, once the office of Jules E. DuBern. He was born in 1857 in France and made his fortune here in 1882 with an ice and mineral water factory. He had his residence in the suburbs near Inya Lake. The road where he lived was once named after him but is now called Maylikha Road.

Across the other side of Sule Pagoda, next to the American Embassy and a few yards off Strand Road, stands what is now the Myawaddy Bank, an elegant building with tall cream yellow Ionic columns shaded by a row of tamarind trees planted in the front. It was built in 1930. It is a shady and secluded spot, an oasis only a few steps away from the mad rush of traffic.

Understandably, because of its position next to the river, Strand Road was the earliest to be developed. Merchant Street, which runs parallel, has always been an important thoroughfare in the city. It boasts the best real estate then and since. Next to the General Post Office, on the corner of Strand and Bo Aung Kyaw Streets, is the British Embassy, once owned by the shipping agents J. and F. Graham and Company. This building was designed and erected at the turn of the century by Robinson and Mundy, the best construction company in Yangôn at the time. J. and F. Graham and Company handled not only shipping and insurance but were also general importers dealing in a diversity of goods, including rice.

The only remnant of the colonial hotel industry in Yangôn is The Strand Hotel. It was owned by Sarkies Brothers, which also owned the Raffles Hotel in Singapore. The Strand opened in 1901 with 60 rooms. The rates at the time were ten rupees a night. It had a billiard room with six tables and a ballroom. It was equipped with its own generator, which supplied the electricity to power its lights and fans. A private artesian well provided water. The kitchen was run by a French chef offering eight-course meals. A roofed pavilion that had once crowned the building has long since been removed. The portico, which jutted out over the front entrance, has been replaced with one that runs the length of the front of the hotel. The Strand has had a colourful social

Right: The Myanmar Independence Monument in Mahabandoola Garden, Yangôn.

history, from the balls and dinners of colonial days and the elaborate wedding ceremonies of post-war Burmese couples to the present-day return to grandeur and old-world charm. High ceilings and long-stemmed fans add to the lazy, leisurely mood. The Australian Embassy across the street was once an annex of The Strand.

Residential buildings from the old days are seen in two distinct forms: the completely western-style home of brick and glass with Tudor or Victorian touches, or timber buildings and spacious bungalows more suitable for the tropical heat. Of the former, three beautiful examples are the main building of the International School, the private residence of a local businessman U San Aung and the headquarters of the Petronas Oil Company. They are all in the area known as Golden Valley, a wooded residential area not far from the Shwedagon.

Most of the residences have retained the traditional and comfortable Burmese design with elevated floors and wide doors that open to spacious verandas. The turn-of-the-century wooden houses owned by the wealthy were mostly two-storey buildings with wide balconies or airy living rooms over the porticoes, slatted doors and delicate friezes of white-painted fretwork along the eaves. Although they are now called Old Burmese Houses, these big timber or half-timber, also called "semi-pucca", buildings have a mixture of native and foreign characteristics.

These homes were comfortable and spacious, and were often set in the centre of lush gardens tended by Indian *mali* or "gardeners". They were the favoured residences of rich merchants and government officials, regardless of race. As protection against termites and harsh weather conditions, the timbers used in these buildings were coated repeatedly with the dregs of crude oil in the manner prescribed by tradition. Since this process resulted in the homes becoming highly flammable, kitchens were set apart from the house and covered walkways were erected to connect them to the back entrance. A steep flight of stairs located at the back of the building provided access for water carriers and Indian sweepers, who would tote bucketfuls of water upstairs to fill the tanks in the bathrooms and carry the pails out from the toilets, respectively.

Opposite, left: *Detail of the former railway headquarters building in Yangôn.*

Opposite, right: *The façade of a bank on Pansodan Street, Yangôn.*

Below: *The Strand Hotel, Yangôn. Note the Doric columns on the ground level.*

The design of Old Burmese houses was strictly symmetrical, both in the ground plans and in the decorative motifs. In the centre of the roof would be a dainty cupola with glass panels, known as the Bengali pavilion, which allowed light to penetrate into the interior. The roofing would be of tiles or more often, wooden shingles. A lacy fretwork border would hang from the eaves with a tapering overhang at the corners. It was usually painted white to stand out in sharp contrast to the dark, natural wood of the walls. The doors and windows were usually arched, with elegant patterns worked into glass, which was either plain or coloured.

The front entrance beyond the wide portico would lead to a narrow lobby with the parlour to one side and a library or music room on the other. Stairs leading to the upper floor would also be in the lobby. Upstairs, the open hallway would lead straight out to the veranda, which is the upper level of the portico. This part of the house would usually be open on all sides or lined with a series of doors and windows set close together. The windows would be flush with the floor and the door flaps of narrow wooden louvres. The door flaps would have been made separately for the top and bottom sections, thus allowing the bottom section to be kept shut for privacy or both

Opposite: *The elegant dining room of the Strand Hotel.*

Left: *The interior of a private residence in Yangôn.*

Above: *The comfortable open veranda of a typical Old Burmese house.*

sections to be opened during the high heat of summer to catch even the slightest whisper of wind. If there were no separate shrine room, the shrine would be set up here in the open hallway. Bedrooms would be located behind or at the sides of this area. Bigger houses would normally have narrow balconies leading out from each bedroom. The partitioning walls would not reach the high ceilings so that there would have been ample space for good airflow.

These timber houses became known as Old Burmese houses although only the roof, with fretwork edging along the eaves and a raised cupola at the apex, resembled vernacular design. Most are sadly the worse for wear, such as the Old Seamen's Home on Prome Road and a house on Po Sein Road that was once the home of the Great Po Sein, the Father of Myanmar Theatre. In somewhat better shape is the Women's Home building on Wingabar Street, which had been donated by an Indian businessman to Daw Khin Hla, a society lady prominent in politics and social welfare work, so she that could set up a home for the orphaned girls she was looking after. One of the best-maintained is the house on Natmauk Road belonging to retired ambassador U Kyin and another is Mira Flores on Pyay Road, which is owned by Daw Kyi Kyi Myint Toon.

Above: *Detail of a cupola on the roof of an old Yangôn residence.*

Right: *Verandas on the upper-level of a home from the colonial period, Yangôn.*

The famed Pegu Club, an immense historical timber building that has fallen into disrepair, was once the bastion of the *Memsahib* with the gimlet eyes, ever on the lookout for those who did not "belong" and those with whom she should cultivate relationships. It is now a government office filled with shelf upon shelf of dusty files in rooms where the Caucasian high society of "Rangoon" dined and danced. Together with the Gymkhana Club, it offered recreational facilities to a select core of colonial society where only friends of one's own race were permitted. As Alister McCrae of the Irrawaddy Flotilla Company pointed out, "it was inevitable in the way our lives were ordered with close European clubs and society. Short of being a rebel, one conformed". The Gymkhana was later turned into a women's hospital.

Almost opposite the Pegu Club on Pyay Road is the Ministry of Foreign Affairs, a neat two-storey building in the colonial style that had been used as a hospital during the Japanese occupation. Some of the long-deceased patients reputedly continue to haunt junior diplomats as they work late. Prettier still and without any ghostly infestation is the Annex building just across a narrow street. It is a jewel of a house, kept pristine with fresh paint all year round.

Below: *An elaborately styled birdcage in the home of Patrick Robert and Claudia Saw Lwin in Yangôn.*

Right: *Replica of a household shrine with a tiered* pyatthat *roof at the Robert residence.*

Opposite: *The living room of the Robert residence.*

Around the corner, behind the other side of Pyay Road, is a beautiful two-storey structure with wide balconies running along both floors of its front façade. The simplicity of the upper pillars with their Ionic capitals gives the building a majestic aloofness that combines with the spare beauty of the Doric pillars on the ground floor. It was built as the residence of the agent of the Imperial Bank of India in 1914. Also known as Bengal House, it was intended to symbolise the full force of British imperial might and thus was designed to be second only to the Governor General's residence. It has a billiard room and a guest room downstairs, while the upper floor has five bedrooms with attached baths. The grounds are extensive. It once had six stables, now turned into two garages and 25 rooms for servants. The floors are of marble and the drawing room floor is of the best teak. The Indian government bought the building in 1955 and it now serves as the Indian Ambassador's residence.

One of the "Old Timber Houses" nearby that has not only been kept in good repair but completely renovated is the Pansea Hotel. The lawns are beautifully-kept and elegant wicker furniture and potted plants fill the dining area on the wide balcony upstairs. With such modern touches as a swimming pool and tiled lotus ponds, the prevailing ambience at this former guesthouse of the Kayah State may not really be that of the slow, dusty days of the past, but it does offer luxurious and beautiful accommodations.

The boat club on the Kandawgyi Lake, once a timber building in the 1880s, was rebuilt and extended several times. After Independence, the rambling brick pavilion with a long veranda "perching its chin on the water", as a Myanmar would say, was renamed the Union Club. During the Socialist years, it was first converted into a natural history museum that had a large model of a dinosaur peering into the upper reaches of the tall trees on the grounds. It was then turned into the Kandawgyi Hotel, one of a few in the whole country at the time. The hotel served sardine sandwiches and weak tea at exorbitant prices.

Opposite: *The Old Seamen's Home, Yangôn.*

Top left: *Mira Flores, an Old Burmese timber house on Pyay Road, Yangôn.*

Bottom left: *Daw Kyi Kyi Myint Toon, owner of Mira Flores, in the garden of her home.*

Right: *The Indian Ambassador's residence in Yangôn, once a symbol of British colonial power.*

Far left: *The Pansea Hotel in Yangôn, a timber-based building, incorporates both local and foreign features in its architectural design.*

Left: *A sitting area in the Pansea Hotel.*

Below: *An open veranda at the Pansea Hotel.*

Now the Kandawgyi Palace, an immense, sprawling timber hotel, it has a new annex that displays a combination of Thai and Burmese architectural styles. The bare wood of the structure, devoid of any trace of crude oil, blends into the lush greenery of trees that may have been on the site when the first clubhouse was built. The dinosaur still resides in the garden, peering at guests taking breakfast on the patio.

Belmont, the British Ambassador's residence, is situated not far from the Kandawgyi Lake, also called the Royal Lake. A few other houses also stand on the compound. The land and houses were once owned by the Irrawaddy Flotilla Company, which had bought ten acres of land near the lake in 1885 and built five houses for its expatriate staff. The present Belmont replaced the old wooden house in 1927. Well-trimmed lawns set off the regal exterior to perfection. Each British ambassador has in turn brought his or her own personal touch to the place, including a pet crocodile and a python.

Left: *Poolside at the Kandawgyi Hotel, Yangôn.*
Below: *Detailed woodcarvings at the Kandawgyi Hotel.*

The mansion has a beautiful, wide stairway curving up from the hall. Its teak-panelled walls gleam with polish. During the time of the Japanese occupation, the building had been used as a military office. One small bedroom on the upper floor was used in 1941 to billet General Aung San and his junior officer, the future General Ne Win[96], for a month. The two had clashing personalities; General Aung San was a strict disciplinarian and devoted family man while his junior was a playboy, and one can only wonder at the amount of tension generated that steamy monsoon month of July.

French windows lead onto the wide verandas. A driveway circles the portico, in front of which stands a bronze statue of Sir Arthur Phayre staring moodily down onto a patch of British soil. It was moved here many years ago from its original location at the Zoological Gardens, a stone's throw away. At the zoo, the statue had stood near a pretty house built in 1915. That house is now called the King Edward VII Pavilion and has been converted to house reptiles.

The Steel Brothers Chummery, a dormitory for young bachelors, was built not far from Belmont. During the riotous time when it housed no less than 18 of Steel's numerous bachelor assistants, it was known as "The Gin Place". After Independence, it was used as a training school for military officers and is at present an up-market hotel complete with a wildly successful nightclub. No doubt, during its term as a military school, it was full of earnest young men oblivious to the beauty of its high pillars and dainty stucco designs.

The residences of the American Ambassador and the Deputy Chief of Mission have a history as enticing as the view they command. Looking out over the placid waters of Inya Lake, they are in the centre of the headland with a total water frontage of 560 yards. The houses had been built by the MacGregor Company in 1930.

A young Scot from Glasgow, John MacGregor arrived in Burma in 1869 and three years later joined the timber and tram company founded by the Englishman, John Darwood. MacGregor soon became a partner but the company split in 1885. MacGregor took over the

Right: *The British Ambassador's residence, also known as the Belmont.*

timber business and Darwood the transportation and electric supply sector. Both were hugely successful, becoming millionaires in a short time. MacGregor was a very prominent figure, serving as the Chairman of the Chamber of Commerce and a member of the Lieutenant Governor's Council. He passed away in 1900, leaving half his huge fortune to the poor of Glasgow and half to the poor of Yangôn.

Thirty years after MacGregor's death, the chairman of his company, John Robertson built the two houses that were sold some 20 years later to the government of the United States of America. The house that is now the American Ambassador's residence was once called Tighnamara. It stands on seven-and-a-half acres of well-kept grounds with beautiful old trees. In addition to the entrance hall, inner hall and a large dining room, it has three large reception rooms on the lower level. The side verandas are enclosed, providing more space for the receptions so essential on The Fourth of July, which happens to be a day in the wettest month of the Myanmar monsoon season.

As in most of the houses built before air conditioning was invented, the house is positioned so that it catches even the mildest breeze during the hot summers. A line of trees protects it from the lashing rains that come from the southwest. Luckily, there is no strong

superstition in Myanmar connected to the direction in which a house is aligned. The lawns are cultivated and clipped to perfection. There is a spacious elevated lawn within a low ornamental wall, two fountains and paved walks. Steps and terraces lead down to the water's edge.

The smaller house of the Deputy Chief of Mission was built in 1938 and named Tighnabruaich. The severe lines of this square building are softened by a covered, semicircular, glass-walled patio. The house sits on its own grounds of two-and-a-half acres, hidden from the bigger residence by a clump of high trees. Some of these trees are magnificent and look as if they have been there since the lake came into being.

Opposite: *A pavillion at the Yangôn Zoo.*

Above: *The American Ambassador's residence perched on the edge of Inya Lake.*

Right: *The American Ambassador's residence, once known as Tighnamara, as viewed from its extensive gardens.*

Pages 166-167: *The only house made of teak in Washington Park, a compound for American diplomats located in Yangôn.*

A long, winding road set deep in the grounds and under the bridges connects the two houses. The road looks as if it had once been a canal fed with water from the lake. As mentioned in Maurice Collis' book, *Lords of the Sunset*, the lake had at one time covered a considerably larger area. He wrote that when he stayed at his friend Noel Whiting's home in 1936, they had to row to shore in a sampan.

Whiting's home, a Chinese-style house on an island in Victoria Lake with a tower 90 feet high, was built by Lim Ching Hsong, a Chinese businessman who had made a fortune in the oil market. After his "palace" was completed, Lim bought a steamer from Bibby Lines, renamed it "Seang Bee" and sailed to England to purchase furnishings befitting of such a residence. He also brought back a Rolls Royce. However, after the death of his beautiful young wife and the loss of half his fortune, Lim no longer had the heart to live in the mansion and sold it to Whiting. Always called the Ching Hsong Palace after the original owner, the tower is now part of the Ministry of Culture. The surrounding area is very much drier than it was 70 years ago, the building being now some hundred yards away from the water. Apparently, the lake has receded over the years.

It is not only in Yangôn that western-style buildings stand with eastern-style ones. Maymyo, named after a Colonel May but now known by its original Burmese name of Pyin Oo Lwin, is a hill station east of Mandalay. It is a small jewel of a town nestled within the folds of several hills, a sanctuary of coolness during the high heat of summer. To the Myanmar, it is known by a poetic name, "Royal Flower City". Many European companies and private citizens located their bungalows and cottages on this hill resort. Not a few of these buildings had non-Burmese sounding names, apparently given by homesick expatriates. Sweet peas, roses, crocuses and lilacs bloom in profusion here along with flamboyant native flora.

Right: *Ching Hsong Palace was named for the original owner, a Chinese businessman who later sold it to Noel Whiting.*

Pages 170-171: *The train station at Kalaw, a popular hill station in the Shan state, with a public transport pony cart.*

Candacraig Hotel in Pyin Oo Lwin once housed the bachelor employees of the Bombay Burmah Trading Company. It is an English country mansion transported through space and time, replete with fireplaces, sweeping stairways and roast beef dinners in the dining room. As a hotel, it no doubt still has roast beef on the menu.

Another cool hill resort is Kalaw but Pyin Oo Lwin, being easily accessible, was more favoured. Many retirees from British companies decided to live out their days in Kalaw or Pyin Oo Lwin. Kalaw, meaning "frying pan" in the language of the ethnic Pao who live in the area, rests like a pan between the high hills.

A house of stone built in 1910 now stands within an army outpost. Noel Whiting, who also owned the Ching Hsong Palace, once lived there. He was a friend of Queen Supayalat and probably the only *kalu hpyu*[97] the old queen received. The house, called the Rock House, with an arched wooden front door giving it added rustic effect, is believed to have been built by a Scot. During his time, snakes living in the foundations were said to frequent the house and were allowed to come and go without harm, domesticated as much as snakes could be. Close to it is a replica of a Scottish shepherd's croft, aptly named "Sentinel".

Other towns were not stations for leisure. They were for work, where companies stationed agents to look after their teak, rice, or transport interests. A town not far from Kalaw, called Taungyi or "Big Mountain" is another popular summer resort but it is not as pretty as the sprawling and wooded Kalaw. Other towns in the Shan States such as Loi Mei and Kyaingtong (Kengtung) boast some examples of pretty architecture, standing unchanged for these long years.

If most of the impressive buildings of the British were offices or residences, the ones built by the Burmese were monasteries. One built entirely in the western style by the minister Kinwun Mingyi U Kaung after his sojourn in Britain and Europe in 1871 still stands in Mandalay. Commonly known as Thaga Wun Kyaung, it is a monastery of wood carved to look as if it were made of brick and stucco, complete with Corinthian columns and an eagle with wings spread atop the windows. It was once painted a pale cream colour to complete the

Left: *Candacraig Hotel in Pyin Oo Lwin, built in a style reminiscent of an English country mansion.*

illusion. The only Burmese touch is lace-like traditional *Kanote* designs carved into the wood panels of the doors separating an inner hall from the portico. To protect the entire wooden structure from fire, U Kaung had a narrow moat dug around it.

Another beautiful monastery, built by the minister U Hpo Hlaing, colleague of Kinwun Mingyi U Kaung, is the Yaw Min Gyi Oke Kyaung. It is a two-storey brick building near Mandalay Hill with Italian designs and Myanmar flora. Yaw Mingyi U Hpo Hlaing was a very able and learned minister who served the last two kings of Burma. He invented the Morse code for the Burmese language in 1869 when the telegraph was first introduced to Burma. In 1878, he wrote a treatise on the ethics of being a ruler and suggested changing the political system in Burma from a complete monarchy to a parliamentary system. The idea was not received positively by the power behind the throne, Chief Queen Supayalat and her mother. The minister was removed from office two years later and spent the remainder of his life writing more treatises.

Only the cream-coloured shell of his graceful monastery remains after the ravages of World War II. One can still see the sweeping flights of stairs, high pillars and arched doorways. Long corridors that circle the immense central hall lead into smaller chambers. The roof is gone; in the harsh sunlight, weeds and wildflowers carpet the ground where once monks had paced and nobles had knelt in prayer.

A strange combination of nature, religion and western architecture is to be found at the Shwe Ba Taung Cave Pagodas in Monywa. Enshrined within are images carved out of living rock. Narrow corridors lead to shallow but high caves with entrances pillared and capped with arches in the colonial style, complete with griffins and unicorns.

Many other colonial-era pagoda pavilions or monasteries with western architecture remain to this day, miraculously untouched by World War II. They can be seen not only in the royal capital of Mandalay but in every town with a flourishing monastic order. Examples would be Sagaing, Pyay, Bago, Thanlyin, Toungoo, Sale, Pakokku, Pyinmana, Pyuntaza, and Yeynan Gyaung, to name but a few.

Right: *Hsipaw Mansion, one of many colonial-era buildings in Shan State.*

Religious buildings were not the only structures to be built in the western style. Two small pavilions in the Mandalay Palace commissioned by King Thibaw also had western influences. One to the south of the Glass Palace was used as his residence, a rather unpretentious white-washed brick building where he liked to spend his days reading or talking to officials he considered friends. Another building, not far from the Watch Tower, had a fountain in the open courtyard and an inner chamber covered with frescos done by two Italian artists serving at the royal court. This painted pavilion was destroyed during World War II but King Thibaw's "home" remained untouched.

With more contractors and craftsmen learning to build in the style of the west, it became increasingly popular to build structures that were a fusion of east and west. Western-styled pillars, gables, trefoil windows and Italian archways were worked into the design of traditional Burmese motifs such as floral scrollwork and tiered *pyatthat*. The exotic combinations were done in such an imaginative way that the results are often charming. One exquisite example is the Ordination Hall of Kyundaw Monastery in Yangôn.

Below: *Detail of a carving atop an archway at the Shwe Ba Taung Cave Pagodas.*

Right: *The design of the Shwe Ba Taung Cave Pagodas in Monywa was influenced by western architectural styles.*

Another stands at the junction of Nawadday Street and Shwedagon Pagoda Road, a small, high, bright red building built in 1910. It is named Kyar Ku Monastery, "Where the Tiger Crossed". This place was once deeply wooded and in 1903, a tigress crossed the road here to head towards the Shwedagon. It then climbed up on the scaffolding in place for the gilding of the spire and rested at the Rim of the Bell. British soldiers came to shoot down the tigress, which the spectators thought was just on a pilgrimage to the pagoda. Instantly, news of the event spread throughout the country through the skits and songs of travelling theatres.

In the compound of the Nga Htut Gyi Pagoda, in the area known as the *wingabar*[98], there is a two-storey brick monastery with European touches and detailed Chinese decorations all picked out in a rainbow of colours. It is a unique mixture not of two but three cultures.

Countries and neighbours have exchanged ideas, concepts and arts through the ages. Whether the exchanges come from near or far, through friendship, business, religion or war, each has contributed to the culture of the other. Thus people can cherish them as relics of the past, for although they were not a part of the country's original culture, they are certainly a part of its history. In Myanmar, standing alongside traditional structures are the architectural heritage of strangers, adventurers, immigrants and invaders. The most amazing results are the combination of these diverse styles, symbolic of the historical melting pot that has helped create the harmony of the present.

Opposite: *Kyundaw Monastery Ordination Hall, located in Yangôn.*

Left: *Nga Htut Gyi Monastery, Yangôn.*

Pages 180-181: *Mayon, the home of Mark Tippets in Pun Hlaing, is an east-meets-west melding of traditional Myanmar elements and modern design aesthetics.*

ENDNOTES

1   To reflect local usage, the official Myanmar names of places have been adopted throughout the text with the colonial names appearing in parentheses at first mention. "Myanmar" is used as a contemporary reference to the country and its people while "Burma" and "Burmese" are used in the historical or ethnic context.

2   The Burma Communist Party and various ethnic groups within the country took part in a number of rebellions against the government. However, the communists were defeated in 1989 and most of the armed ethnic groups made peace agreements with the government at approximately the same time.

3   "Pagoda" is a term used herein to refer generally to a place of worship, be it a stupa or a temple.

4   The biggest uncut stones are easily more than 600 carats in size.

5   A 70-foot-long jade boulder with a 35-foot circumference was found in the Hpakant mines, 40 feet underground.

6   Approximately eight per cent of the population is Christian, five per cent Hindu and Islamic, and two per cent animist.

7   Meaning "summit" in Sanskrit, a stupa is a mound-shaped edifice. It is also referred to as a *zedi* in Myanmar.

8   The shape of the "umbrellas" is based on the Magait crown worn by Burmese kings on coronation and state occasions.

9   The origin for the word *gu* can be traced to the Sanskrit word *guha*, meaning "a hidden place".

10 In the Burmese language, *lemyethna* means "four-faced".

11 Inhabitants of a few villages deep in the Maha Myaing forest around Monywa district claim to be of Pyu descent. They use several archaic Burmese words.

12 The common name for the large, golden-yellow fruits (*Cyttaria darwinii*) that grow in clusters in southern South America.

13 A Burmese measure of weight still in use today. One *viss* is equal to approximately 3.6 pounds.

14 Bazaars.

15 A British civil administrator during the colonial era in Myanmar, later to become famous as a writer.

16 *Thein* usually refers to an ordination hall used solely by monks or men, but here it is used as a name for a pagoda.

17 The various parts being the trunk of an elephant, eyes of a doe, horn of a rhinoceros, tongue of a parrot, body of a carp, tail of a peacock, ears of a horse, mane of a lion and fangs of a tiger.

18 Stories of the 550 former lives of the Buddha.

19 In the Burmese language, *Andaw* means "royal molar".

20 Crowned images found elsewhere in Myanmar are based on a *Jataka* story of the Buddha showing a king the futility of wealth.

21 1) To be charitable. 2) To be virtuous. 3) To favour with gifts. 4) To be gentle. 5) To practise the eight Buddhist precepts. 6) To have no anger. 7) To conform to the wishes of monks and men. 8) To be easy with taxation. 9) To be forgiving. 10) To be just.

22 The British called it "Akyab", probably after the Agyat Pagoda, which was located on its shore.

23 In July 1975, an earthquake damaged many of these structures. Some small temples were reduced to rubble.

24 *Nat* are spirits of men and women who died violently. Bitter and unhappy with their fate, they cannot be reborn into other spheres of existence. Caught in limbo and malevolent if crossed, these spirits are worshipped because they can grant favours. Two other kinds of *nat* are celestial beings and animistic guardian spirits.

25 Groups of letters from the 33 Burmese alphabets are assigned to each day of the week, beginning with Monday. The days are counted from Sunday, so it has the number one, while Monday is two and so on. Each word of this rhyme corresponds to a number and in order they read 4,446. Personal names are also chosen according to the day on which one is born. There are no surnames in the Burmese tradition.

26 According to a UNESCO report of 1988.

27 The sap is fermented as wine that is drunk the same day, as it does not keep, or is cooked down into palm sugar.

28 Theravada is a school of Buddhism practised in Myanmar, Thailand and Cambodia. Mahayana is practised in Tibet, China, Japan, Korea and Nepal. Theravada focuses more on the teachings of Gautama Buddha and meditation for self-awareness while Mahayana has more mystical and ritualistic aspects to it, including the worship of the *Bodhisattva Maitreya*, the Future Buddha *Maitreya*.

29 Many scholars believe the invasion to be a matter of fact as a tale about it was inscribed in stone 400 years later by another Mon king named Dhammazedi.

30 Molds of stone or metal were used to form clay into tablets onto which were inscribed scenes from the *Jataka* or the Buddha's life story.

31 In Buddhism and Hinduism, *samsara* refers to the continuous and repetitive cycle of birth, suffering, death and reincarnation one has to go through in the quest to attain Nirvana.

32 Many of these places were broken into and looted centuries ago.

33 "Seven parts of *ohnton* plant, nine of glue from buffalo hide, two of molasses and half from the *ohnshit*, or "bael", tree. A handful of cotton and a ladleful of oil."

34 A few successive kings, during whose reigns the architectural style changed to Burmese, sometimes reverted to building pagodas in the Late Mon style. Thus, it is not possible to determine the architectural style of a structure strictly according to chronology.

35 The Lacquerware Museum of Bagan is in possession of a bowl dating from the same period.

36 Discovered near the Tharapa Gate, it is presently being housed in the Bagan Museum.

37 A many-tiered roof that culminates in a pointed apex, seen only on royal and religious buildings.

38 Unfortunately, a great fire that broke out in Bagan in April 1225 destroyed all the wooden buildings in the city, including the palace.

39 Known erroneously as the Myazedi Stone as it was discovered in the early twentieth century near a pagoda of that name.

40 An ancient recipe states that the cement was made from one part *kyazu* (*Terminalia citrina roxb.*), one part molasses, three parts *ohnshit* (*Aegle marmelos correa*), six parts glue from buffalo hide, 22 parts *ohnton* (a tree of *Litsea* species), to be dried, pounded and mixed again with buffalo hide glue four times. It did not state which parts of the trees were used.

41 "U" is the male prefix to a name for monk and men. "Ko" is used for young men, and "Maung" for boys. "Daw" is a female prefix. "Ma" is for young women and girls. These prefixes are never used for those who are of royal blood.

42 The original was totally destroyed by the earthquake of 1975 and a replica was built on the site.

43 Some *nat* are religious teetotallers and some are patrons of drinkers and gamblers. One *nat*, a little girl who died at the age of three, looks after babies' welfare.

44 Myanmar has a ceramic legacy unlike that of any other country in the Southeast Asian region. In 1984, some green and white ceramic ware of a type that had never been seen before were discovered at an ancient burial site in the town of Tak in Thailand, near the Myanmar border. A series of tests revealed that the lead isotope ratios of these shards matched only those of glazed ceramic ware found in

the temples of Bago and Bagan. The difference between the glazing process in these samples and the glazed wares of other Southeast Asian countries was the addition of tin to the lead flux to whiten the colour. Ceramics experts have found this attribute to be unique to ancient Burmese technology.

45 Chapter XLII. Of the Manner in which the Grand Khan effected the Conquest of the Kingdom of Mien and Bengala.

46 Mount Meru.

47 The Lion Throne, with figures of lions on the pedestal. The other thrones, each made of a different wood, were the Bee, Lotus, Deer, Elephant, Peacock, Conch Shell and Hamsa Bird Thrones. There were two Lion Thrones, bringing the total number of thrones up to nine. All but one of the Thiha Thana Thrones were destroyed during World War II. This throne, symbolising the centre of the Earth in traditional Burmese belief, is now in the National Museum of Yangôn but is not under a nine-tiered roof.

48 A Mon princess and a widow at 29 when she was presented to the king of Inwa, she eventually escaped to Bago and ruled the Mon kingdom after the death of her elder brother. She was a great supporter of the Shwedagon Pagoda.

49 Also similar to the ceremonies for the construction of another palace in Mandalay 349 years later.

50 He who would be a Future Buddha.

51 Her complete title is A Lair Nan Madaw, meaning "Queen of the Central Palace". The title of the Chief Queen, "Queen of the Southern Palace" was reserved for princesses of true royal blood.

52 Puppeteers could say what others could not since technically the dolls were the ones speaking. In this manner, many things were reported to the king without the need for the bearers of bad news to be punished. The marionette stage even managed to poke fun at the powerful Nan Madaw queen Mai Nu, no mean feat.

53 Stories of his debates with the king, who often came out the worst for it, are still reprinted and read.

54 *Ain-gyi Thakin* or *Ain Shay Thakin*, meaning "Master of the Great Front Residence", are terms used to address the crown prince in the first person. A different term, *Ain Shay Minthar*, "Prince of the Front Residence", is used to refer to the crown prince in the third person.

55 One day each week, determined according to a lunar calendar, was considered to be a religious fasting day as well as a holiday. This tradition is still observed in many places in Myanmar.

56 The bearer seemed to be reporting to the king who was in his own apartments as there was an interval between messages.

57 *Mandalay Myo Nan Ti Sar Dan* by Sithu U Maung Maung Kyaw.

58 Buddha, His Scriptures, and the Order of the Sangha.

59 Who share the same birthday as King Mindon.

60 Linear measurements are often still calculated according to paces, the distance from the elbow to the tip of the middle finger (one *taung*; approximately 18 inches) and the distance between the tip of the thumb and the tip of forefinger when the two are splayed wide apart (one *htwar*, approximately nine inches).

61 The neighbourhood is now respectable.

62 432 pounds.

63 Diamond, ruby, pearl, coral, cat's eye, emerald, topaz, sapphire and garnet. They are also set in rings to be worn by men. They must be set in a certain order with the ruby in the centre.

64 The question of whether human sacrifice occurred is still debated. An eminent historian has even suggested digging up the foundations to settle the question once and for all.

65 Such pathways are used only by monks or highly-placed personnel.

66 The First Synod was held by the Buddha's closest disciples, Ashin Kassappa and Ashin Annanda, three months after his passing to ensure that his teachings would be recorded correctly. The second was held a hundred years later. After another hundred years, King Asoka held the Third Synod. The fourth was held two hundred years after that, and King Mindon held the fifth. The Sixth Synod was held by Prime Minister U Nu in Yangôn from 1954 to 1956.

67 The quarry is still operating today. In 2001, it yielded the biggest marble block ever be found. It was brought to Yangôn and carved into an image, the Yangôn Kyauktaw Gyi or the Lawka Chantha Abhaya Labha Muni, "Prosperity to the Universe and Protection from Harm", image.

68 Prince Kanaung happened to be testing a bomb in the palace lake at the same time that King Mindon offered food to the abbot. On hearing the explosion, the abbot had refused to eat, saying that he felt sad for the creatures in the lake killed by the bomb. There and then, King Mindon ordered any use of explosives stopped.

69 The massacre was ordered by the dowager queen and a number of ministers. It was carried out by King Thibaw's trusted right-hand man, Prince Yanaung, great granduncle of the author of this book.

70 On the main Thiha Thana Throne, the king sat facing east while the queen was seated south of him, to his right. Other queens were not allowed to sit on this most noble of thrones.

71 Supayagyi was a good poet and sent King Thibaw many messages accusing him of treachery. He replied to them with apologies but she never forgave him. Her poems are quoted to this day.

72 The pregnant girl was executed by Supayalat who had apparently chosen to disregard the belief that to kill the unborn child of a king would mean the end of the royal dynastic line.

73 It has been translated into English by L.E. Bragshawe and is published by Orchid Books, Bangkok, Thailand. ISBN 974-524-021-4 (hb).

74 As part of a scheme against her mother two years before, Queen Supayalat had given her youngest sister, Supayalay, to King Thibaw to be the third queen.

75 A replica of the palace was built on the original site in 1995.

76 Some accounts say the clothes were burned and the ashes mixed with lacquer. It is a rare royal custom to have one's clothes dipped with lacquer and moulded into images. Another tradition is to mix the dried and powdered petals of certain flowers with the lacquer. This "Blend of a Thousand Blossoms" clay is considered a sacred material. The flowers were picked on auspicious days at auspicious times and dried in the shade, for the hot rays of the sun supposedly represent the heat of suffering. The use of this clay, which is time consuming to prepare, has been discontinued.

77 It has since been rebuilt.

78 1) Painting. 2) Sculpting. 3) Blacksmithing. 4) Metal-casting. 5) Decorative motif stuccowork. 6) Turning or woodworking. 7) Marble- or stone-casting. 8) Masonry. 9) Crafting with precious metals. 10) Lacquerware-making.

79 The rules included regulations concerning the height and width of the steps to the front door and the requirement that a large bush of *galon let thair* (*Polyscias fruticosa*), a plant used as a cure for sexually transmitted diseases, be planted in the front yard.

80 Animals are usually housed in sheds in the backyard and not kept under the house.

81 A yellowish paste ground from the bark of a tree (*Limonia accidissim linn*) used as makeup for women and children.

82 Papers by Myo Myint Sein et al, Rangoon Institute of Technology, 1970, and research done by U Sun Oo Aung Myint, CEO, Design2000.

83 A high tone is the *ma* or female voice, the low one the *hpo* or male.

84 The colonial era was rife with rebellion. After independence, there were constant battles with the Burma Communist Party and ethnic nationalist groups that lasted well into the late 1980s.

85 Such as those found at Lawka Hteik Pan and Myinkaba Gubyaukgyi temples, among others.

86 Monks who have gained more enlightenment and are certain of attaining Nirvana.

87 The Buddhist monastic order.

88 The last time a *hti* was completely replaced was in 1871, merit of King Mindon. Yangôn was under British rule and the king himself was not permitted to come to Shwedagon so he sent ministers in to represent him for the occasion.

89 His body, dried but not decayed, can be seen in a glass coffin in a pavilion at the far end of the compound.

90 Many westerners have the misconception that the Myanmar themselves use "Burma", "Rangoon" and other Anglicised names. Only a Myanmar who speaks English would recognise these names.

91 Kings were married to their half-sisters to keep the bloodline pure, resulting in many an odd behaviour in their offspring.

92 In what is now Chinatown.

93 A gesture of respect to images of the Buddha as well as monks and elders performed by removing one's footwear, kneeling on the floor and bowing three times with hands clasped together. A less formal version involves bowing from the standing position with one's hands clasped and footwear removed.

94 Father of Daw Aung San Suu Kyi, noble laureate and leader of the democratic movement of 1988.

95 It was nationalised in 1964, two years after General Ne Win took power in a *coup d'etat* and forced-marched the country along his disastrous "Burmese Way to Socialism".

96 He took power in 1962 but his Socialist government was overthrown in 1988 by the democracy movement led by General Aung San's daughter Daw Aung San Suu Kyi.

97 "White Indians" as westerners were called.

98 Labyrinth.

SELECTED BIBLIOGRAPHY

Myanmar Language Publications

Aung Kyaing, Minbu. *Bagan Khit Pi Thu Ka Let Yar Myar* (Bagan Era Architecture). 1st ed. Yangôn: Sarpay Beikman, 1985.

Aung Kyaing, Minbu. *Let-yar Sone Swar Ananda* (Fine Works of the Ananda). 1st ed. Yangôn: Sarpay Beikman, 1987.

Kala, U. *Maha Yarza Win Gyi* (The Great Chronicle). Yangôn: Hanthawaddy Press, 1962.

Khin Khin Su, Daw, ed. *Pi Thu Ka Kyan* (Text on Architecture). Yangôn: Burma Research Society, 1966.

Maung Hsu Shin. *Myat Paya Shwedagon* (The Glorious Pagoda Shwedagon). Yangôn: Sarpay Beikman, 1972.

Maung Maung Kyaw, Sithu, ed. *Mandalay Myo Nan Ti Sar Dan* (Record of the Building of Mandalay). 1959.

Maung Maung Tin, U, ed. *Kon Baung Set Maha Yarza Win Daw Gyi,* vols. 1, 2 and 3 (Great History of the Konbaung Dynasty, vols. 1, 2 and 3). 4th printing. Yangôn: Sagawar Sarpay, 1989.

Maung Maung Tin, U, ed. *Kon Baung Set Maha Yarza Win Daw Gyi,* vol. 2 (Great History of the Konbaung Dynasty, vol. 2). Third printing. Yangôn: Lehdi Mandaing Press, 1967.

Maung Maung Tin, U, ed. *Kon Baung Set Maha Yarza Win Daw Gyi,* vol. 3 (Great History of the Konbaung Dynasty, vol. 3). Third printing. Yangôn: Lehdi Mandaing Press, 1968.

Maung Than Swe (Dawai). *Konbaung Shin Dan* (Explanations of Konbaung) 1st ed. Yangôn: Yar Pyei Sar Oke Taik, 2001.

Maung Than Swe (Dawai). *Shay Taw Win Hmat Tan Myar* (Records of Visits to the Royal Presence). 1st ed. Yangôn: Yar Pyei Sar Oke Taik, 2003.

Min Htin Raza, Kanni Sittke. *Mandalay Yadanabon Maha Yarza Win Gyi* (Great History of Mandalay). 1st ed. Mandalay: Tet Nay Lin Press, 1969.

Mya Kay Tu. *Nan D'lei Hmat-tan Myar* (Record of Royal Rituals). 1st ed. Yangôn: Hna Lon Hla Sarpay Publications, 1966.

Myint Than, Daw, *et al.* Myanmar Sar A Hpwei, U Si Htar Na (Committeee for Myanmar Language Affairs, Supervising Department). *Hman Nan Maha Yarza Win Daw Gyi,* vol. 1 (The Glass Palace Chronicles, vol. 1). New edition, 1st printing. Yangôn: Ministry of Information, 1992.

Myint Than, Daw, *et al.* Myanmar Sar A Hpwei, U Si Htar Na (Committeee for Myanmar Language Affairs, Supervising Department)). *Hman Nan Maha Yarza Win Daw Gyi,* vol. 2 (The Glass Palace Chronicles, vol. 2). New edition, 1st printing. Yangôn: Ministry of Information, 2003.

Myint Than, Daw, *et al.* Myanmar Sar A Hpawei, U Si Htar Na (Committeee for Myanmar Language Affairs, Supervising Department). *Hman Nan Maha Yarza Win Daw Gyi,* vol. 3 (The Glass Palace Chronicles, vol. 3). New edition, 1st printing. Yangôn: Ministry of Information, 2003.

Myo Myint Sein, U, U Hla Myint, U Kyaw Thein, U Sai Yi Laik, U Nan Wai (artist, University Translation and Publication Department) and students. Department of Architecture, Rangoon Institute of Technology. "Konbaung Khit Hnaung Hpone Gyi Kyaung Myar" (Monasteries of the Later Konbaung Era). *Tekathoe Pyinnya Padetha Sarsaung Journal,* vol. 5, pt. 4. Yangôn: Universities Translation and Publication Department, 1970.

Myo Myint Sein, U, U Hla Myint, U Kyaw Thein, U Sai Yi Laik, U Nan Wai (artist, University Translation and Publication Department) and students. Department of Architecture, Rangoon Institute of Technology. "Shay Myanmar Ein Myar" (Traditional Myanmar Houses). *Tekathoe Pyinnya Padetha Sarsaung Journal,* vol. 5, pt. 4. Yangôn: Universities Translation and Publication Department, 1970.

Myo Nyunt, U. *Bagan Khit Pahto Myar Pi Thu Kar Hnit A Nu Let Yar* (Temples of the Bagan Era: Architecture and Details). 1st ed. Yangôn: Ministry of Culture, 1999.

Po Hmat Su, Yadanabon. *Mandalay.* 1st ed. Mandalay: Kyee Pwar Yay Press, 1946.

Su, U. *Myanmar Yoe Yar Pithu Kar A-swan* (Traditional Myanmar Architecture). 1st ed. Yangôn: Sarpay Beikman, 1986.

Thiri Uzana, Wungyi, Inyon Ywar Sar. *Lawkabyuhar Kyan* (*Inyon Sardan*) (Rituals and Traditions of the Myanmar Kings). Edited by U Po Lat. 3rd printing. Yangôn: Ministry of Culture, 2001.

Tin Naing Toe. *Myanmar Yarza Wun Ei Thamaing Kyaung* (Myanmar Historiography). 1st ed. Yangôn: Pyei Sone Publishing House, 2001.

Tin Win Myint. "Pyatthat Myar Ko Le Lar Chin" (A Study of Pyatthat). *Traditional Architecture Series*, no.1. Yangôn: Research Department, Ministry of Construction. 1994.

Zeyar Thingaya. *Shwebon Nidan* (Introduction to Court Rituals). Edited by Hla Thamein. 3rd reprint. Yangôn: Hanthawaddy Press, 1963.

English Language Publications

Aung Thaw, U. *Historical Sites in Burma.* 1st ed. Rangoon: Sarpay Beikman, 1972.

Aung-Thwin, Michael. *Pagan: The Origins of Modern Myanmar.* Honolulu: University of Hawaii Press, 1985.

Ba Shin, Bohmu. *The Lokahteikpan: Early Burmese Culture in a Pagan Temple.* 1st ed. Rangoon: Burma Historical Commission, 1962.

Ministry of Culture, Burma. *The Mandalay Palace.* 1st ed. Rangoon: Directorate of Archaeological Survey, 1963.

Collis, Maurice. *Into Hidden Burma.* Reprint. London: Faber and Faber, 1954.

Collis, Maurice. *The Land of the Great Image.* 2nd ed. London: Faber and Faber, 1953.

Ferras, Max and Bertha. *Burma.* 1st ed. London: Sampson Low Marston, 1901. Reprint, Bangkok: Ava Publishing House, 1996.

Grant, Colesworthy. *Rough Pencillings of a Rough Trip to Rangoon in 1846.* Calcutta: Thaker, Spink and Co., 1853.

Htin Aung, Maung. *A History of Burma.* New York: Columbia University Press, 1967.

Kelly, R. Talbot. *Burma Painted and Described.* London: Adams and Charles Black, 1905.

Luce, Gordon. H. *Old Burma: Early Pagan,* vol. 1. New York: J.J. Augustin, 1969.

McCrae, Alister. *Scots in Burma: Golden Times in a Golden Land.* 1st ed. Edinburgh: Kiscadale Publications, 1990.

McCrae, Alister and Alan Prentice. *Irrawaddy Flotilla.* 1st ed. Paisley, UK: James Paton, 1978.

Pearn, Bertie R. *History of Rangoon.* 1st ed. Rangoon: Rangoon Municipal Corporation, 1939.

Scott O'Connor, Vincent C. *Mandalay and Other Cities of the Past in Burma.* London: Hutchinson, 1907. Reprint, Bangkok: Ava Publishing House, 1996.

Singer, Noel F. *Old Rangoon: City of the Shwedagon.* 1st ed. Stirling, Scotland: Kiscadale Publications, 1995.

Shwe Zan, U. *The Golden Mrauk-U: An Ancient Capital of Rakhine.* 1st ed. Yangôn: Rakhine Thahaya Association, 1994.

Symes, Michael. *Journal of His Second Embassy to the Court of Ava in 1802.* Edited by D.G.E. Hall. 1st ed. London: George Allen and Unwin, 1955.

Than Tun. *Twenty-one Tales of Bagan Bago Awa.* 1st ed. Mandalay: Htipaungkar Books House, 2002.

Tun Shwe Khine. *A Guide to Mrauk-U: An Ancient City of Rakhine, Myanmar.* 1st ed. Sittway: Sittway Degree College, 1993.

Wright, Arnold, ed. *Twentieth Century Impressions of Burma: Its History, People, Commerce, Industries and Resources.* 1st ed. London: Lloyd's Greater Britain, 1910.

Yi Yi, Daw. "The Thrones of the Burmese Kings". *Journal of the Burma Research Society,* vol. 43, pt. 2, December 1960. Yangôn: Burma Research Society, 1960.

Index